THE
GENESIS
OF A
HUMANIST
MANIFESTO

by

Edwin H. Wilson

edited by

Teresa Maciocha

THE GENESIS OF A HUMANIST MANIFESTO

by

Edwin H. Wilson

edited by

Teresa Maciocha

HUMANIST PRESS
AMHERST, NEW YORK 14226

*Funds for the publication of this book
were provided through a grant
from the
James Hervey Johnson
Charitable Educational Trust*

Printed and bound in the United States of America.

Library of Congress Catalog Card Number: 95-08056

ISBN 0-931779-05-7 paperback

CONTENTS

Preface

About the Author

Edwin Henry Wilson was born on August 23, 1898, in Wood-haven, New York. He was raised in Concord, Massachusetts, where he attended the First Parish Church, a Unitarian fellow-ship. Wilson's father had no use for the church; it was his mother who introduced him to Unitarianism, albeit of the conservative variety.

During World War I, Wilson served in the Army Signal Corps. In 1922, he received a bachelor's degree in business administration from Boston University. After a brief period as a sales manager, he returned to school in 1924 to attend the Meadville Theological School, at that time located in Meadville, Pennsylvania, and exclusively Unitarian. (The school moved to Chicago in 1928. Meadville had a long-standing relationship with Universalist Lombard College—a relationship which was formalized in 1964 when the name was altered to the current Meadville Theological School of Lombard College.) Wilson graduated from Meadville in 1926 with degrees as a graduate of divinity and doctor of divinity, after which he spent a year abroad as a Cruft Fellow, studying at the Sorbonne in Paris.

Following his ordination in 1928, Wilson became a practicing Unitarian minister in Dayton, Ohio, where he eventually became minister emeritus. Over the next sixty-five years, he had pulpits in Schenectady, New York; Chicago, Illinois; Yellow Springs, Ohio; Salt Lake City, Utah; and Cocoa Beach, Florida.

Throughout his life, Wilson maintained a dedication to learning, but it was during the period when he was a matriculated student that he became exposed to and convinced of the validity of the humanist outlook. His conviction that "humanism has time, science, and human need on its side" proved to be life-long.

Ed Wilson's humanist career began in 1929 when he became a regular contributor to *The New Humanist*, then a mimeographed newsletter published by the Humanist Fellowship in Chicago. Primarily composed of students from a number of universities and colleges in the Chicago area—in particular, the University of Chicago—the fellowship was a forerunner of such humanist organizations as the American Humanist Association. By 1930, Ed Wilson was the managing editor of the publication (no longer mimeographed but printed) as well as one of the co-owners.

Nineteen hundred thirty-three was a milestone year for Wilson. It marked both the publication of "A Humanist Manifesto" in *The New Humanist* and the beginning of his fifty-two year marriage to Janet Wilson. The Wilsons had two sons, John and Dana.

When *The New Humanist* ceased publication in 1936 due to lack of funds, Wilson continued to spread the humanist message with his own modestly produced *Humanist Bulletin*. In 1941, that was succeeded by *The Humanist*, still in publication today. Wilson served as editor of *The Humanist* for sixteen years (consecutively from 1941 to 1956 and then as interim editor for a period between 1963 and 1964). In addition to editing and contributing to *The Humanist*, he was also one of the founders of the American Humanist Association, incorporated in 1941, and served as its executive director from 1949 to 1970. Subsequently, he was a member of its board of directors and was named the association's official historian.

In 1952, Wilson participated in the founding and naming of the International Humanist and Ethical Union (based in the Netherlands), uniting the humanist movement worldwide. He remained an active member for forty years.

Wilson's dedication to humanism earned him much respect and many honors. In 1955, he was awarded the American Humanist Association's Humanist Merit Award. In 1978, he received the Distinguished Service Award, the Unitarian Universalist Association's most prestigious honor to the cause of liberal religion. And in 1979, he was named the AHA's Humanist of the Year.

Early in his career, Dr. Wilson contributed to the body of humanist liturgy by collecting hymns and services, even writing a hymn called "Where Is Our Holy Church?" During a 1987 interview with Beverley M. Earles (currently an officer of the American Humanist Association, but at that time a doctoral student of religious studies), Earles asked Wilson how he thought he'd be remembered. Wilson laughingly replied that most likely it would be as the composer of that hymn.

Dr. Wilson was a primary author of both *Humanist Manifesto I* (originally published in 1933 as "A Humanist Manifesto") and *Humanist Manifesto II* (1973). He knew that both the consensus process of creating the first manifesto and its publication were significant events worthy of recording in this book, which he wrote over the course of many years during the 1970s and 1980s.

Wilson remained a fierce advocate of religious humanism his whole life. In the interview with Earles, she reported to Wilson that she had heard said of humanists: "They're atheists who can't quit the habit of going to church." To this somewhat lighthearted challenge, Wilson responded that he thought churchgoing "was a good habit. It organizes one's life. It's where your friends are. I find a great deal of stimulation in the institution of continuing education." In fact, Wilson always equated the humanists' quest for greater knowledge while striving toward the ideal of a "good life" as a form of continuing education.

A productive and vigorous man all his life, Ed Wilson died in Salt Lake City, Utah, on March 26, 1993, at the age of ninety-four.

Introduction

The Genesis of a Humanist Manifesto is Edwin H. Wilson's story of how the humanist manifesto of 1933 was shaped, how it came to have thirty-four prominent endorsements, how it was published, and, ultimately, its historical impact. Wilson writes from his position as one of the originators of the project —a man who chose to live and work his entire life by his commitment to the manifesto's principles.

Dr. Wilson recorded the events surrounding the 1933 manifesto some forty to fifty years after they occurred, and he died before a publisher had been secured. This decades-long lag time can be partially explained by Wilson's prodigious career as a professional humanist: for most of his life he was simply far too busy to write his memoirs. I think, too, that the passing decades eclipsed Wilson's recollection of the significant socioeconomic and political conditions of the 1920s and 1930s which contributed to the growth of humanism and precipitated publication of "A Humanist Manifesto." The reader will find few references, and then only in passing, to these conditions. Wilson seems far more preoccupied with honoring his colleagues who played a role in the development of humanism. He seems also to have a secondary agenda of acknowledging the legitimacy of humanism throughout this century and thereby repudiating those who would or did dismiss it.

In 1933, the United States continued to be in the depths of the Great Depression. Franklin Roosevelt had just taken office (March 1933), so the New Deal had not yet arrived. The effects of economic disparity were evident everywhere, and fascism was rising rapidly in Europe. There were several generations who remembered clearly the pain and horror of World War I. Socialism, in its theory and as it was being practiced in the Soviet Union, still held for many great promise as a potential (and legitimate) way to address economic disparity. Science, the scientific method, and their offspring—technology—were changing forever the agrarian foundation of the United States. What's more, this triumvirate had provoked a kind of hopefulness for bettering the world out of all proportion to its fallibility as a human system. For humanists at that time, science seems to have been sacrosanct.

In preparing his 1954 doctoral dissertation *Making the Manifesto: A History of Early Religious Humanism*, William Schultz spent ten days as a guest of Ed Wilson and conducted extensive interviews with surviving manifesto signers. In the course of his research, Schultz examined the work of several of the philosophers of that era, including John Dewey (a manifesto signer) whose work, among many other things, delves into the nature of knowledge and action. Schultz observes that Dewey's philosophy came

> on the explosive heels of the technological revolution, it quite readily reinforced the "rumor" already spreading for several decades (since Huxley's time and before) that science could transform Being. Man was flexing his muscles in Nature's face; intelligence, judgment, and the scientific input could regulate and direct her. Lacking the obstacles which a deity might provide, and confident that the universe (matter) was just waiting to be exploited for man's benefit, humanity stood in awe before the possibilities with which its new Weltanschauung presented it. Religious humanism institutionalized that awe.

By the 1930s, religious (or naturalistic) humanism had developed within and without liberal religions—in particular, Unitarianism—so that the time seemed right for a number of its advocates to write and publish a manifesto that would capture the essentials of this religion or philosophy. Their desire to promote and advance humanism should not be ignored. While publicity may not have been the preoccupation in 1933 as it would no doubt be today, the idea of promotion was still there. In 1933, the natural vehicle for such promotion was *The New Humanist*, a bimonthly magazine published in Chicago, a hotbed for humanism in the early part of this century.

The project was initiated by Raymond Bragg, one of the leading young Chicago-based Unitarian advocates of humanism, who enlisted an author for the first draft as well as a small editorial committee, which included Edwin H. Wilson, another of those young Unitarian movers and shakers of religious humanism.

While Unitarianism was not the only source for the growth of humanism, it was central. Given that Ed Wilson was an ordained and practicing Unitarian minister, it is from this perspective that he wrote *The Genesis of a Manifesto*. That fifteen of the thirty-four men who signed the manifesto in 1933 were Unitarians poses a difficulty for any who might dispute the importance of Unitarianism in the development of the humanist movement.

To be sure, humanism was developing outside the liberal religions as the reader will discover upon reading the pre-eminent names of men of science, letters, and academia covered in the following chapters.

In his 1964 book, *Religion in Twentieth Century America*, Herbert Schneider attempted to characterize humanists:

> There are among the humanists left-wing Unitarians who do not reflect the liberalism of Emerson and who do not wish to be confined to Christian limitations. There are materialists who are no longer "doctrinaire" materialists but who are suspicious of the theologians who use terms like "soul," "immortal," "transcendental," "God," and "spirit"; they prefer more secular language for their secular truths. There are naturalists who are disgusted by the use of . . . supernatural symbols and myths . . . who find no use for organized religions, but who have a "religious" concern for the life of reason. There are still a few old-fashioned rationalists, free-thinkers or professional atheists. . . . And there are many individuals who cannot be labeled. . . .

Whatever else may be said of religious humanism in the third decade of this century, it wore a mantle of hopefulness about humankind's ability, through intelligence, to rise above all obstacles. This hopefulness is spelled out in the manifesto's fifteen points. Charles H. Lyttle, a Unitarian historian who, in 1952, chronicled the events of liberal Unitarianism, including the development of humanism, corroborates this point when he said that the manifesto "sought to replace despondency and doubt of God's loving Providence by confidence in the power of human intelligence and co-operative good will to become its own Providence."

Acknowledgements

As editor, I wish to acknowledge the following people who have been most helpful and generous with their time in the postmortem editing of Dr. Wilson's manuscript:

- Various librarians, Buffalo and Erie County Public Library, Main Branch, Buffalo, New York
- Bette Chambers, president emeritus, director of planned giving, assistant to the president, and editor of *Free Mind*, American Humanist Association, Amherst, New York
- Karen D. Drickamer, curator of manuscripts, special collections, Morris Library, Southern Illinois University, Carbondale, Illinois
- Beverley M. Earles, vice-president, American Humanist Association, Amherst, New York
- Frederick Edwords, editor of *The Humanist* and executive director, American Humanist Association, Amherst, New York
- Karen Ann Gajewski, associate editor and production manager, American Humanist Association, Amherst, New York
- Neil Gerdes, librarian and historian, and members of the staff at Meadville-Lombard Theological School Library, Chicago, Illinois
- Carolyn Kemmett, public information assistant, Unitarian Universalist Association, Boston, Massachusetts
- Emma Lapanski, Society of Friends archivist, Haverford College, Haverford, Pennsylvania
- William F. Schultz, who gave permission to obtain a copy and quote from his 1975 doctoral dissertation, *Making the Manifesto: A History of Early Religious Humanism*, in partial fulfillment of the requirements for the doctor of ministry degree from the Meadville Theological School

at Lombard College. Dr. Schultz is currently the executive director of Amnesty International and served, from 1985 to 1993, as president of the Unitarian Universalist Association.

— *Teresa Maciocha*

About the Editor

Teresa Maciocha is a freelance editor currently residing in Buffalo, New York, and holds a bachelor's degree in political science from the State University College at Brockport, New York. In addition to her years of editorial experience, she has spent many years working for social change agencies in Washington, D.C., including Community Jobs and Greenpeace. More recently, she worked for the Buffalo Coalition for Common Ground and the Western New York Peace Center in an alternatives to violence program.

CHAPTER 1

"A Humanist Manifesto" — A Historic Document

When thirty-four individualists agree upon anything, it is an unusual event—especially when there is a preponderance of ministers involved. Even though "reasonable minds at work on the same or similar facts" are presumed to arrive at similar conclusions, this is not always the case. Yet in 1933, such an agreement was reached in a declaration of the theses of religious humanism and was published in the May/June issue of *The New Humanist* (VI:3).

In the same issue in which this declaration, "A Humanist Manifesto," was published, an article entitled "Religious Humanism" by Roy Wood Sellars (author and professor of philosophy at the University of Michigan at Ann Arbor) announced the following:

> In the *Humanist Manifesto* it will be seen that many of us have reached a common body of beliefs and attitudes, beliefs about man, his place in the universe, the general nature of that universe, and attitudes toward the great questions of life. . . .

"A Humanist Manifesto" brought to public attention for the first time a movement deeply rooted in the cultural life of the United States of America. This movement has been variously called religious humanism, naturalistic humanism, scientific humanism, and ethical humanism according to the varying backgrounds and emphases of its proponents. In this book, I use the term *religious humanism*, as did the signers of "A Humanist Manifesto." In addition to the varieties of humanism current at that time, historically there have been many humanisms as well. But the humanism announced in the manifesto had "new" horizons; it looked—perhaps too trustingly—to science as the putative savior of humanity. Therefore, "A Humanist Manifesto" should be regarded as but one outcropping of a cultural trend that existed at that time in many places and which since has surfaced in many traditions and nations beyond sectarian barriers.

The 1933 manifesto issued a challenge in the name of naturalism to the supernaturalists whose beliefs were based upon revelation rather than reason and science. It was a bold move to them publicly that their religious views were out of date and that the time had come for a new faith and a new religion. Such a challenge is just as appropriate today in view of the influence of the radical religious right.

The making of this historic document reflected the hope and directions of an era. "A Humanist Manifesto" represented a tide which the fundamentalist Christian revival set out to stem. It may be that Christian fundamentalism will become as obsolete as the particular expressions of the Social Gospel in Protestantism which it engulfed, and that the Christian right will one day discover that time, science, and modern values are not on their side. I believe their own numbers and importance have been inflated by skillful use of the media and by abundant conservative financing. Moreover, the claim that "humanism is dead" (or that "God is dead," for that matter) is a little like the shout: "The king is dead! Long live the king!"

In the mean time, as this century's decades have elapsed, humanists have held dialogues with Marxists and Roman Catholics. Faith in human potential and the stirring of freedom are still shaking the structure of totalitarian regimes, both political and religious. "A Humanist Manifesto," although perhaps with too easy optimism, foreshadowed the revolution in faith and values astir in society today and is a historic and meaningful document.

The pendulum will swing in religion as in politics from the humanistic to the reactionary and theistic, but religious humanism has confidence that it will repeatedly swing back to a new and more broadly based global faith in humanity. There is no return to the values and mores of an agrarian Golden Age. The need for global cooperation to avoid nuclear destruction demands solutions with a contemporary focus.

Throughout this book it should be borne in mind that the founders of the Humanist Press Association, later reincorporated as the American Humanist Association, never intended to establish a church or denomination. Their organization was an aligning for mutual education of persons who belonged to various organized religions or to no organized religion. At the start, those who termed themselves *religious humanists* predominated, but the door was always open to unchurched freethinkers and rationalists.

Some writers have dealt with humanism as a religion, but in its inclusive sense it is also a philosophy and an ethical way of life.

CHAPTER 2

The Background of Religious Humanism

The history of religious humanism in the twentieth century, as it appeared in North America, has yet to be adequately written. The modern humanist movement emerged from liberal religious change at the end of the previous century and the beginning of this one. The influence of the Enlightenment, Charles Darwin, and biblical criticism encouraged liberal trends in Unitarianism, Universalism, the Ethical Societies, and Reformed Judaism. A growing literature reflected the influence of evolutionary thought, especially in the rejection of the Bible as the source of "revealed" truth.

In the last years of the nineteenth century, religious radicals and independents gravitated to an organization known as the Free Religious Association, which was an effort to align those humanistic religious liberals, including freethinkers and rationalists. Ralph Waldo Emerson was its first president and it included among its members Felix Adler, the founder of the American Ethical Societies, plus a few others we can identify as forerunners of our evolutionary, naturalistic humanism. Some could properly be called humanistic theists; they kept theistic terms but redefined them. The Free Religious Association never went beyond what it called *humanistic theism*, and, because of the intense individualism of its members and gathering of dissenters, its exciting meetings— usually front-page newsworthy—soon ended.

In 1951, a Boston humanist named James V. Grasso discovered a reference to the Humanistic Religious Association of London, with a constitution dated September 1, 1853. Eighty years before "A Humanist Manifesto" was published in the United States, local needs had produced religious humanism in organized form in England:

> In forming ourselves into a progressive religious body, we have adopted the name "Humanistic Religious Association" to convey the idea that Religion is a principle inherent in man and is a means of developing his being towards greater perfection.
>
> We have emancipated ourselves from the ancient compulsory dogmas, myths and ceremonies borrowed of old from Asia and still pervading the ruling churches of our age.

Grasso noted in his article, "Humanism in the Eighteenth Century," published in 1951 in *The Humanist:*

> The objectives of the Association were to spread the knowledge of the time and to foster the cultivation of the sciences, philosophy and the arts. The group recognized the individuality, independence and equality of members, and established an electoral system for officers, which provided the vote for each member, male or female, at the age of 18.
>
> The group provided for universal education of children, mutual assistance for those in need (provided that they were unable to help themselves), for the appointment of qualified speakers and teachers, and for social and cultural meetings. Their objective seems to have been to better the members as a whole through education of both children and adults, without neglecting the fine arts and worth-while social intercourse. The association would, they hoped, become "a high school for the people" and would help "form the groundwork for a higher period of cultivation."   [11:4:175–176]

Unitarian Progression

Critical thinkers sought to maintain the integrity of their inward processes, both intellectual and spiritual. This involved a continual process of bringing religious language and objectives into harmony with advancing knowledge and ethical insights. At all times, the writing and thinking of liberal clergy interacted with the academic world—humanistic philosophers, socially conscious scientists, and historians of religion. The way for humanism in Unitarianism had been opened when the measures and foundations of truth and morality were placed outside of the Holy Bible and within human reason and moral conscience. Thus, as Unitarianism grew, religious humanism began to appear long before proponents had a name for it. By its rejection of revelation, religious humanism was inherently opposed to biblical literalism, dogmatism, and religious creeds.

The Unitarian establishment, mostly in the East, called itself Unitarian Christian. Dissenters were represented by the Western Unitarian Conference. In the late nineteenth-century, a controversy ensued (known as the "Issue of the West") over whether there would be a Unitarian creed to exclude nontheists and other post-Christian dissenters. (Professor Charles Lyttle has told this story in detail in his 1952 book, *Freedom Moves West.*) The Western Unitarian Conference stood steadfastly opposed to creeds. For example, William Channing Gannett, a minister at St. Paul, reportedly stated that he wanted the basis of fellowship in his church to be so broad that even the well-meaning atheist would be welcome.[1]

Year after year at the annual meetings, the "creed" and "no creed" forces fought over a verbal formula. Successive efforts to establish a creed for Unitarians have always brought forth an escape clause to the effect that neither the statement

---

1. This statement by Dr. Gannett, a forebear of the Gannetts who founded a newspaper chain, was reported by Dr. Charles H. Lyttle to be in a sermon series entitled *The Four Seasons.* My perusal of this book did not reveal the quote, and some argue that Gannett's true position was less open. However, his wish to welcome all, including nonbelievers, may have been fact. In his book, *A Year of Miracles* (Boston, MA: George H. Ellis Company, 1882), Gannett wrote: "It is hard to prove a God; harder to prove him our God; harder still to prove our immortality." And Dr. Arthur Foote, while ministering at St. Paul in 1973, insisted that the statement about welcoming even atheists would be consistent with Gannett's life work, noting, "It is clear that William Channing Gannett had no desire to make belief in God a requirement for membership."

being considered nor any other statement could be used as a creed with which to exclude people from membership. This precaution is directly reflected in both "A Humanist Manifesto" (1933)—also known as "Humanist Manifesto I"—and "Humanist Manifesto II" (1973). Both documents assert that they are not creeds.

As early as 1909, the Reverend Frank Carlton Doan had set forth in *Religion and the Modern Mind* a humanism centrally concerned with inner experience and self-awareness, but in relation to this-worldly objectives. Doan used the psychology of his day but, unlike the literary humanists and some religious mystics, he did not make his exploration of the subjective an inward retreat from reality or an escape from the social struggle for progress. Rather, the subjective was to him the imaginative and inspired source of ideals pointing to action in the outer world. Doan used the terms *humanism* and *modernism*.

In 1918, Roy Wood Sellars published *The Next Step in Religion*, in which he specifically pointed to religious humanism as "the next step." In Sellars' view, humanism (this-worldly) was sharply contrasted with supernaturalism (other-worldly). He wrote: "Humanism always flourishes when peace and contentment are abroad, and humanism is the deadliest enemy that superstition has to meet."

Curtis Reese and John Dietrich

In that same year, the Reverend John H. Dietrich of Minneapolis and the Reverend Curtis W. Reese, of Des Moines, Iowa, both Unitarian ministers with an orthodox background, confronted their fellow Unitarians with a challenge that could not be avoided. While Reese was speaking at a meeting of the Western Unitarian Conference in Des Moines on "The Religion of Democracy," Dietrich pointed out: "What you are calling the religion of democracy, I am calling humanism."[2] It was a momentous convergence of minds—and at that

---

2. Reese's talk was later published as *A Democratic View of Religion* by the American Humanist Association as Publication No. 218, Leaflet Series.

moment, a movement was launched. Consequently, Reese changed the title of his book to *Humanism*. As Reese once put it, the idea of God was held to be "philosophically possible, scientifically unproved and religiously unnecessary."

A later address by Reese at a meeting sponsored by the Harvard Summer School of Theology in July 1920 brought the issue to a head. Reese and Dietrich's adversaries—including William Lawrence Sullivan, a former priest, and George R. Dodson of St. Louis—wanted the humanists ousted from the denomination. The controversy was described as a battle between the "God Men" and the "No-God Men." But it was the evolutionary theists—the theistic liberal ministers—who defended Reese and Dietrich. The "Issue of the West" and subsequent denominational struggles led the Unitarians to reject a dogmatic creed and to extend the commitment to freedom for the pew to freedom for the pulpit. Humanists were henceforth in the Unitarian movement by right, and that right, implicit in the professed creedlessness of the denomination, was gradually upheld. (If that freedom had not been confirmed, there probably would have been a separate humanist church.)

Interestingly, some of the Unitarian clergy who defended the rights of humanists, such as Dietrich and Reese, to fill Unitarian pulpits were evolutionary theists—that is, they declared that evolution was God's way of creation. The humanists, in contrast, did not suspend their relationship to the cosmos on the language of theism but came out frankly as nontheists.

Curtis Reese and John Dietrich continued to write. Dietrich published his sermons in a series of seven or eight volumes called *The Humanist Pulpit*. His sermons were also widely distributed as pamphlets which helped to spread his fame. Dietrich was a superb artisan, but his sermons often drew heavily upon the thinking of others. However much he borrowed his thoughts—though sometimes without quotation marks or acknowledgement—he always improved on them with a forceful clarity.

In 1927, Reese collected the views of eighteen other Unitarian ministers in a volume entitled *Humanist Sermons*.

In this book, the movement was not merely more obvious but more aggressive as well. A few of those appearing in *Humanist Sermons*—John Haynes Holmes and Frederick M. Eliot, in particular—subsequently changed their views and probably regretted their participation. While Dr. Eliot was never a doctrinaire humanist, he was considered somewhat of an ally. In fact, when he later ran for the presidency of the American Unitarian Association, he was attacked by his opponent, the Reverend Charles Joy, for being a humanist. Not wanting another divisive theological battle, the denomination persuaded Joy to withdraw, and Eliot won the election. In 1944, in the midst of his term (1937–1958), Eliot rejected the candidacy of Curtis Reese for the presidency of Meadville Theological School. Those of us who had perceived Eliot as sympathetic to humanism were disappointed. In correspondence with Reese, Eliot explained that his opposition to Reese's candidacy was not personal but, rather, that Eliot did not want Meadville to be perceived as having fallen into humanist hands.

This disappointment aside, Curtis Reese continued throughout his life to be a leader in the humanist movement. He was one of the primary editors of "A Humanist Manifesto" in 1933 and served on the board of directors of the American Humanist Association for many years. I had always thought him prolific, but it was late in my life before I came to fully appreciate his personal struggle. In 1980, Reese's surviving son (Curtis, Jr.) and daughter (Rachel Sady) sent me a forty-page transcript of the letters sent to Curtis, Sr., by his family, all devout Southern Baptists. To a person, everyone in his family declared that they would rather see Reese burn in hell, as he surely would, if he left the Baptist Church at Tiffin, Ohio, and became minister of the Unitarian Church at Alton, Illinois, as he did. Though Reese had read and thought his way out of fundamentalism, he refrained from responding to the end of the year, at which time he wrote a letter to an unidentified member of the family with a dignified and reasonably objective refutation that barely concealed the hurt and alienation he must have felt. In the interim, his sister, who had previously named her son for Curtis, legally changed the child's name to that of a Baptist evangelist. Reading that correspondence, I understood for the first time the painful pressure that had produced the terrific productivity and dynamic leadership of Curtis Reese.

I believe there is a recurrent historical error that creeps into articles written since the 1980s—namely, the references to either Dietrich or Reese as the "father" of humanism. In fact, modern humanism is multifaceted; it is not a one-person, one-book movement but, rather, a globally oriented plateau with new leaders and advocates emerging from various cultures.

With this in mind, credit must be given where it is due. By aligning a whole group of Unitarian ministers, Curtis Reese foreshadowed a humanist organization. He was a creative innovator and organizational guide of early religious humanism. John Dietrich and, after him, T. C. Abell, Charles Francis Potter, and E. Burdett Backus were among the movement's popularizers.

Additional Efforts at Organizing

Humanism began to spread within (and beyond) the Unitarian denomination as well as to other liberal religious groups. Indeed, early efforts at the institutionalization of humanism came in the form of groups schismatic from Unitarianism. In fact, two ministers who signed the manifesto made early attempts at humanist organizations by withdrawing from Unitarian congregations and starting independent humanist societies. One short-lived effort was attempted in 1933 by Dr. Eldred V. Vanderlaan of Berkeley, California. The other— the First Humanist Society of New York—was begun in 1929 by Dr. Charles Francis Potter, who, for a number of years, financed his venture through his writing and lecturing, as well as from collections and contributions from a group of sponsors he developed—a group which included such distinguished people as Albert Einstein.

The second issue of the printed (not mimeographed) *New Humanist* in January/February 1931 had an announcement of the First Humanist Society of New York on its back cover. Also that year, Dr. Potter's book, *Humanism: A New Religion*, was offered in combination with a subscription to *The New Humanist* (along with other books, including Robert J. Hutcheon's *Humanism in Religion Examined*). The Reverend A. D. Faupel withdrew a following from the Oakland, California, Unitarian church which, as far as we know, had always had a theistic minister. Faupel's schismatic movement eventually obtained its own building and, as the Fellowship of Humanity, became the first and oldest affiliate of the American Humanist Association. The fellowship is still in existence.

Another California group, the Hollywood Humanist Society, was organized by the Reverend Theodore Abell around the same time as the New York organization. The editors of *The New Humanist* had repeatedly sought Abell's cooperation and financial support; however, he declined all invitations whether they were to write or review a book or even to join the Humanist Press Association. We regretted his disinterest very much as we had heard that he was doing a vigorous and competent job in the Los Angeles area, broadcasting regularly and building up a considerable personal following.

When Raymond Bragg and I were developing a list of potential signers for the manifesto, we said, "Let's not invite him to say 'no' again." This decision was a mistake. I learned years later that Abell would have liked to have been asked to sign the manifesto. Of course, this was when it became obvious that the document was historic. I think it is not improbable that Theodore Abell adopted an attitude that one often encounters among the "prima donnas" of any movement: in this case, *L'humanisme c'est moi!* (roughly translated, this means, "Humanism is mine" or "I am humanism").

Abell published a local periodical for the Hollywood Humanist Society, which he called *The Humanist*. I learned many years later that he felt *The New Humanist* had purloined his publication's name. Relations with Abell were not improved in 1941 when our publication changed its name from *The New Humanist* to *The Humanist*.

In due time (after I had moved to Salt Lake City, Utah, in 1946), Abell and I met and were able to bury our animosities with direct and friendly communication. I always regretted the strained relations between us and attributed them to inadvertent factors of too great distance and not enough communication. I view Theodore Abell as a real humanist pioneer.

In 1933, the Reverend Gordon Kent—another Unitarian schismatic pioneer—started a Humanist society in Moline, Illinois. He had a reputation for certain sensational and erratic tendencies, such as dimming the lights with a rheostat during his meditational services and easing the lights back on when he got to the "Amen." Though he may not have been regarded as sufficiently respectable, Kent's paperback *Humanism for the Millions* went through numerous (and large) editions as a conscious effort to reach the hypothetical "man on the street."

It should be noted that, in his meditations, Gordon Kent was capable of soaring flights of poetic prose quite in contrast with his occasional crudities. He was not unlike another humanist, Hugo Robert Orr. While Orr produced some exquisite sonnets with emotional impact, his public speaking and organizational work moved toward harsher, secular, iconoclastic, and almost anti-religious extremes.

In 1946 and for a time after, Orr conducted the San Francisco Humanist Society, generously subsidized by John Danz, a moving-picture theater owner from Seattle, Washington. Danz wanted a sharp break between organized humanism and the Unitarian movement. He probably realized that that church was a chief competitor of local humanist organizations. Ethnically Jewish, Danz wanted "humanist temples" and held a rather oversimplified concept of humanism. In 1946, he tried unsuccessfully to get me to leave the Unitarian movement to organize such temples. Eventually, the John Danz Foundation financed an annual humanist lecture in Seattle. Hugo Orr's work with the San Francisco Humanist Society ended and was succeeded by a formal chapter of the American Humanist Association.

How I Came to Humanism

Born into a Unitarian household, I had been christened in the First Unitarian Parish of Concord in 1898, where, as my father said, "the people worship God Almighty half the time and Ralph Waldo Emerson the other." I graduated with a business degree, and my undergraduate training was qualitatively deficient in the humanities. But, as a fledgling sales manager, I had observed the passing on of ignorance and superstition from generation to generation in Catholic and fundamentalist churches. As a leader of a college-age Sunday evening youth group of the Second Unitarian Church in Boston, I had been bombarded with questions about the various meanings of God and religion by students from the colleges and universities in the area. Group discussions led me to think of the liberal church as an educational instrument for change.

As I was leaving Boston for the Unitarian Theological School, then still in Meadville, Pennsylvania, Martha Everett St. John, widow of Charles E. St. John, my mother's cousin, warned me, "Don't let those humanists at Meadville take away your faith." That defensiveness shocked me. It was the first time I had encountered the term *humanism.* I had recently heard Unitarian Sanford Bates, the U.S. prison commissioner (as I recall), state that "there is not one belief that I hold that I would not change on five minutes' notice if I ran into a new fact." Then, in an Erie Railroad smoking room, I was confronted by a midwestern professor of philosophy who said, "What a shame for a bright young man like you to be throwing his life away on a dying profession." Those were fighting words for me at that time, and it was a long night. I was still a product of the Unitarian Christian establishment, though with growing mental reservations.

Generally, the strategy of the liberal religious traditionalists in dealing with change was to ignore it. Humanism was usually a forbidden word in establishment talk. How a religious organization deals with change is one test of its ultimate integrity and its adaptation to changing needs in a changing world. In 1927, I interviewed Alfred Loisy in Paris. Loisy was the excommunicated leader of the modernist movement in Roman Catholicism. He showed me a thrice-edited manuscript containing a philosophy of religion which the modernists had hoped to use as a replacement for the thought of Thomas Aquinas. "All we wanted," said Loisy wistfully, "was to have the church accept the fact of change." But that's another story. Unitarians have done well with change. Tolerance and pluralism are built into its creedlessness.

At the Meadville school, as I climbed the stairs to my assigned room in Divinity Hall, I encountered three students who had packed their bags and were already leaving at the beginning of the term. In answer to my question, "Why?" I was told, "We are humanists and the faculty has made it clear that our presence is not appreciated." Three good men were lost to the liberal ministry: one to become a professor of anatomy; one, a professor of English; the third, ultimately, president of a liberal college. Today this would not happen.

But this was January 1924. In the months following, I did all my required class work, but I spent my own time avidly reading everything about humanism that I could lay my hands on. By mid-June, I had said to myself, "That is it! Humanism has time, science, and human need on its side. I'll stick with it!" It proved to be a lifetime commitment. The school was eventually moved from Pennsylvania to a site adjacent to the University of Chicago. Because of my growing doubts, I hedged by taking some sociology courses in the university as a possible alternative career. But I was turned off by behaviorists who disclaimed any compassionate interest in how their research was used and by graduates in sociology who were planning to go into private industries as advisers to profitmakers. A lecture by L. L. Bernard, entitled "The Transition to an Objective Standard of Social Control," especially turned me off. Humanity got that objective social control under Hitler.

I then sought an interview with Dr. Curtis W. Reese. He helped me reach the conclusion that I could best serve my goals in the liberal ministry.

Preceding the Manifesto

Over the following years, here and there a rabbi or an Ethical Culture leader took on the label of *humanist*. A sudden spate of books and articles—pro and con, written by some of the era's finest scholars—began to appear. Echoes of the Scopes trial were still in the air, the Great Depression was ongoing, and the New Deal had not yet been born. And the principal political hope to many persons of humanist and humanitarian outlook (which are, of course, two different things) was found in the leadership of Norman Thomas, who advocated a democratic, non-Marxist form of socialism, or in refrains from labor leader Eugene Debs or journalist and reformer Henry George. (It was also the era of Harry Emerson Fosdick and Christian Modernism.) The time seemed ripe to "break the dead branches from the past." It was to be done largely within the existing liberal churches and not by schism. "A Humanist Manifesto" in 1933 was a principal expression of the movement.

CHAPTER 3

The New Humanist —
Sponsor of the Manifesto

The *New Humanist* was started in 1927, while I was study-ing in Europe as a Cruft Fellow, an award for graduating seniors. The first issue—volume one, number one—appeared in 1928. Examination of the brief record of this periodical preceding the publication of "A Humanist Manifesto" will explain much. Little magazines come and go, but this one was destined to last. Originally, there were three mimeo-graphed volumes, followed by five printed volumes. After a brief lapse between 1936 and 1941, the magazine resumed publication with a new format in the spring of 1941. The new publication was called *The Humanist* and continues to this day. Publishing for over sixty years under its various titles, clearly this periodical has a message of substantial import.

I was editor of *The Humanist* for fifteen consecutive years, until the March/April 1956 issue. I briefly resumed editorial responsibility late in 1963 through the end of 1964. After I retired from this position, Priscilla Robertson, Gerald Wendt, Tolbert McCarroll, Paul Kurtz, Lloyd Morain, David Alexander, Rick Szykowny, and Don Page served successively through mid-1993. During Paul Kurtz's tenure, *The Humanist* became the jointly sponsored publication of the American Humanist Association and the American Ethical Union. In 1978, the AEU withdrew as co-publisher, a new charter was drafted, and Lloyd Morain was elected editor.

Several of those who were active in the initial years of

The New Humanist were students of Dr. A. Eustace Haydon, professor of comparative religions at the University of Chicago. Dr. Haydon had followed George Burman Foster in that chair, as he had also followed Foster in the pulpit of the Unitarian Church at Madison, Wisconsin, for weekend preaching. Moreover, Canadian-born Haydon (whose background was Baptist) had taught humanism in a men's class at the Hyde Park Baptist Church in Chicago. In Canada, he had attended McMaster University in Hamilton, Ontario, where he knew industrialist Cyrus Eaton, who was also a student there. Eaton was an early supporter of humanism. He and Haydon were lifelong friends.

It would be difficult to measure the influence of Dr. Haydon on his students. Some years later, at one of my wife's Oberlin class reunions, I met Professor Walter Horton and asked him how it was that he had so promptly and knowledgeably answered the humanist challenge. He replied that Union Theological School had sent him to Chicago to take Haydon's classes and learn "what was going on out there." It turned out that what "was going on" was scholarly based inspiration. Students reacted strongly to Dr. Haydon, with both favor and disfavor.

At that time, there was a deluge of humanist scholarship. With Dr. Haydon's encouragement, the students in Chicago from both Meadville and the University of Chicago, plus some adjacent schools, organized the Humanist Fellowship and *The New Humanist* was published, originally as a mimeographed bulletin. In more than one financial crisis, Dr. Haydon himself paid for the mimeographing.

When *The New Humanist* first appeared in April 1928 as "a Bulletin of the Humanist Fellowship," breadth rather than exclusive dogmatism was the mood. In the opening statement of the publication, H. C. Creel, president of the fellowship, wrote:

> The membership of the Fellowship is not, at present, limited to persons of any single type of interest or any single walk of life. It is hoped that, as it grows, this will continue to be the case. Humanism, to be worthy of its ideals, neither

can be a neo-ecclesiasticism nor a neo-scholasticism. We are interested, primarily, in building a society in which every human being shall have the greatest possible opportunity for the best possible life. Insofar as we are Humanists, every secondary interest must be judged by this prime criterion.

Creel stated editorially in the second issue of *The New Humanist* that the purposes of the Humanist Fellowship and its publication included an effort to bring "the Humanists of this country (and of the world, if possible) into relations of mutual awareness and cooperation." The magazine also sought to answer the need of humanist churches for service materials. To meet this need, a column, "The Humanist Pulpit," was introduced in the second issue of the publication and was edited for a brief time by Harold T. Lawrence and A. Wakefield Slaten until April 1929 when I took it over. This marked the beginning of my continuous involvement in humanist writing, editing, and publishing.

Harold Buschman, who had written for *The New Humanist* from its start, became its editor in December 1929. In addition to producing a scholarly journal, one of Buschman's goals was to discover and publish young writers of promise. Names which later became well known in the academic world began to appear in the publication, including Edwin E. Aubrey, Theodore Brameld, Hadley S. Dimock, A. E. Haydon, Walter Horton, Frank H. Knight, Douglas Clyde MacIntosh, Wilhelm Pauk, Werner Petersman, Roy Wood Sellars, Matthew Spinka, and Henry Nelson Wieman.

There were theists among these writers, clearly indicating that the editors of *The New Humanist* were not drawing dogmatic doctrinal lines but, rather, exploring religious humanism in dialogue with its critics, as well as giving voice to its advocates. The Reverend Harvey Swanson, then a Unitarian theological student who later became one of the most outspoken opponents of humanism among the ministers, set forth his criticism of "humanism without God" in early issues of *The New Humanist*. Years later, at Swanson's church in Lancaster, Pennsylvania, the laymen's group invited me to speak to them on humanism, which I did while a mighty-voiced and indignant Swanson, speaking before another group on the other side of a folding door, all but drowned me out with his stentorian thunder.

In the April 1929 issue of *The New Humanist*, there were several articles in which I found evidence of applied humanism in a committee of the American Philosophical Society (Philadelphia), which was seeking to bring together "purely scientific interests and the humanistic interests" in an effort to relate biology, psychology, psychiatry, medicine, law, and the social sciences with an understanding of human behavior.

Beginning in January 1930, I shifted from editing "The Humanist Pulpit" to a new column called "The Humanist Movement," which dealt with humanist trends found in secular culture beyond all churches. I discovered the diffused, then-unnamed secular humanism in modern society which would later arouse the likes of evangelists such as Jerry Falwell. Over the course of the following year, my column covered many dimensions of "Humanism—A New Synthesis": "Among the Intellectuals," which included the Institute of Human Relations at Yale University (January 1930); "The Development of Method in Cooperative Problem Solving," citing a program of the American Medical Association (February 1930); "The Organization of Knowledge" in libraries and encyclopedias (March 1930); and "Integrating Science to the Popular Mind," which cites efforts and methods of the American Association for the Advancement of Science to popularize science (April 1930). I also pointed to adult education in England and the United States as evidence that what is now called *secular humanism* was beyond authoritarian church control (May and June 1930).

Also in 1930, Harold Buschman asked me to become managing editor of the publication, which really meant raising funds, putting together the material the editor had gathered, and getting it printed. Already a minister at the First Unitarian Church in Dayton, Ohio, I accepted the management on condition that, rather than mimeo, *The New Humanist* become a printed publication. Buschman agreed.

A thick file of ensuing correspondence between Buschman and me, now housed in the Humanist Archives at the University of Southern Illinois at Carbondale and at the national office of the American Humanist Association in Amherst, New York, indicates our conflicting and interacting goals and values. Some humanists felt that the very strength of humanism was in its diffusion in the world's culture and that for it to manifest itself in a visible organization would lead to its suffocation by critical reaction. (This perception received partial justification by the politically oriented right-wing fundamentalists of the 1980s.) However, I believe that, if the Bill of Rights stands, the suffocation will not occur.

I wanted organization—not only to be able to pay the printer but to spread humanist ideas. Buschman wanted a good, academic journal. There is much to be said for his position. He was neither an organization man nor a fundraiser, but bills had to be paid. My aim was principally to get more readers for the men whose ideas I believed had time, science, and human need on their side—ideas that were opposed to the cultural lag, the entrenched financial position, and the vast numbers of adherents of the revealed religions. I had been inspired by James Harvey Robinson's *The Humanizing of Knowledge*. The pamphleteering and book-selling of the Rationalist Press Association was also in my mind. As an organizer and promoter, I sought to be "Man Friday" to the idea-men who deserved a far greater hearing.

Buschman brought men to the staff who later went far in other pursuits—Alexander Cappon and Clarence R. Decker (who helped Buschman edit *The New Humanist*) and later joined him on the faculty of the University of Kansas City. There, under the editorship of Cappon, they produced the excellent academic journal that Buschman wanted, the *University of Kansas City Review.* Cappon became a professor of English; Buschman, a professor of philosophy; and Decker, an administrator who subsequently became president of Farleigh Dickinson University in New Jersey.

The high standards that Buschman and his colleagues set for *The New Humanist* account in no small part for its continuance and for the distinction of its contributors. Graduating from its mimeographed format, the first printed volume appeared in November 1930 (IV:1) and continued as a bimonthly. The publication began to spread to college and university libraries (bound copies are rare but can be found in the Humanist Archives). Although the Humanist Fellowship disappeared mysteriously from the scene, the magazine survived and flourished. The fellowship apparently folded so quickly and quietly that I was unable to trace it, even in the memories of some of its surviving founders.

From 1930 through 1934, Harold Buschman and I privately owned and published *The New Humanist*—an ownership necessary to obtain second-class mailing privileges. No formal or incorporated humanist organization then existed to take on the responsibility of publication. None of the several churches or churchmen who were trying to set up schismatic (Unitarian) humanist societies along church lines tried to establish a national organization. On paper, the New Humanist Associates was formed—persons privileged to help meet printers' bills.

Buschman's move to New York City to work with the Ethical Culture Society resulted in the associate editor, Raymond B. Bragg, and myself being chiefly responsible for getting the magazine out during 1933 and 1934. In 1935, Bragg, then secretary of the Western Unitarian Conference, officially succeeded Buschman as editor.

Such is the background of the journal that published "A Humanist Manifesto" in 1933. The publication office was then at the Western Unitarian Conference, 105 South Dearborn Street, Chicago. A subscription cost one dollar a year.

In 1935, ownership of the publication was assigned— along with the copyright of "A Humanist Manifesto"—to the newly organized Humanist Press Association, the successor to the Humanist Fellowship. The HPA became the first organized national association of humanism in the United States. Originally inspired by the Rationalist Press Association, the HPA, on the suggestion of Curtis W. Reese, reorganized later as the American Humanist Association. Incorporated in 1941, the AHA became the principal organization representing humanism in the United States. After some years in Yellow

Springs, Ohio, its offices were moved to San Francisco, then in 1978 to Amherst, New York. Copyright of "A Humanist Manifesto" was transferred to (and permission to reprint must now be obtained from) the American Humanist Association (P.O. Box 1188, Amherst, NY 14226-7188).

CHAPTER 4

"A Humanist Manifesto" — The Beginning

R aymond B. Bragg, as the associate editor of *The New Humanist*, initiated the project that resulted in the 1933 publication of "A Humanist Manifesto." In a letter dated February 17, 1970, reminiscing about the early stages, Bragg wrote: "The fact is that my job as Secretary of the Western Unitarian Conference allowed me to move about to see people and to talk with them. It was a convenient post under the circumstances."

As he traveled about on his work for the conference, a number of people urged him to issue a definitive statement about humanism. Bragg writes in the same letter:

> I believe the first person to discuss with me the importance of some kind of humanist blast was L. M. Birkhead.[1] Charles Francis Potter was also insistent that something be done, though he had in mind a more popular thing, such as appeared in his book.[2] I believe it was in 1931 when I appeared at his first and last Annual Humanist Conference [in New York] that he discussed the matter

---

1. Leon M. Birkhead was minister for many years at the Unitarian Church of Kansas City, Missouri, and organizer of Friends of Democracy, an organization which exposed the American fascists, including such Christian fundamentalists as Gerald L. K. Smith. A friend of Sinclair Lewis, Birkhead was Lewis' technical adviser for the classic, *Elmer Gantry*, and a signer of "A Humanist Manifesto."
2. Charles Francis Potter, *Humanism: A New Religion* (New York: Simon and Schuster, 1930).

with me. Once discussed, you may recall, some of us felt that something ought to be done about it. . . .

The fact is that in academia there was fear of a merely journalistic or promotional approach. I can remember a crass example of commercialism with a man named Howard Kraus, who appeared in Minneapolis and wanted to promote humanism on a commission basis—much the same as the Ku Klux Klan had been promoted. Harold Buschman responded to Klaus' proposal by remarking, "That stinks!" Raymond Bragg also remembered being visited by Kraus at his Chicago office. "He talked about promoting humanism by endorsing various commodities, including contraceptives," Bragg recalled.

We may judge that fear of a shallow, unethical, or insensitive approach by someone was no small part of the motivation that led Bragg and others to start the project. Within the humanist movement, there was none of the drive or opportunism of the fundamentalist spell-binders described by Alan Bestic in *Praise the Lord and Pass the Contribution*. The televangelists of the 1980s had their prototypes from some years before.

When Raymond Bragg undertook the organizing of "A Humanist Manifesto," he was only thirty years old. He had been educated at Bates College in Lewiston, Maine, where there was a Unitarian geology professor who was successfully opening his students' eyes to the primacy of scientific inquiry. Having explored Unitarianism himself, Bragg decided to enter the theological school at Meadville, Pennsylvania. In 1926, he moved with the school to Chicago, where he became exposed to humanism under the tutelage of Dr. A. Eustace Haydon, Curtis Reese, and others. Bragg graduated from Meadville in 1928 and went on to a two-year ministry in Evanston, Illinois. He then moved back to Chicago to take the post as secretary of the Western Unitarian Conference.

Further recollections of the start of the project are found in a letter from Dr. Bragg to Dr. A. E. Haydon, dated March 3, 1971:

When I was Secretary of the Western Unitarian Conference, driving from one end of the land to the other, several

individuals talked to me about issuing a resounding statement that would put the Humanist position on the line.
As an itinerant, it was thought that I could stop off here
and there, seeking light and leading. There was also, I suspect, the fact that I had a full-time secretary when such
a commodity was rare. There was a negative aspect to the
enterprise. Charles Francis Potter was talking rather loudly
about such a statement. Some had doubts as to whether
the description of the movement should be left to him.
Charles, as you recall, had some slap-dash quality regretted
by not a few. In fact, I think you cautioned me against drawing too heavily on Potter.

To be fair, it should be stated that I did not fully share
these apprehensions about Charles Francis Potter. After years
in Unitarian churches, Dr. Potter gave his time and effort for
still more years to lecturing at the First Humanist Society
of New York without recompense; he earned his living by
lecturing and writing—no small achievement. On occasion
he protested to me against being considered a popularizer just
because he could write so that the layperson could understand him. My respect for him grew with years of association, and before Potter died, he pointed to a shelf of books
and documents and told his wife Clara "not to let anyone touch
them until Ed Wilson took what he wanted for his library."
Moreover, Potter cooperated fully with the project Bragg initiated and gave helpful advice on press releases and other
publicity. By indicating that Dr. Potter was a catalyst, building
fires under the meticulous academic men and stirring them
to action, no disrespect is intended for his memory nor lack
of appreciation for his unquestioned and unique contribution
to the humanist movement. He put humanism in the headlines
before "A Humanist Manifesto" was written.

Twenty years after the publication of the manifesto, Bragg
wrote "An Historical Note," which appeared in the March/
April 1953 issue of *The Humanist* as part of a symposium.
He said:

For a year or more prior to the publication of the Humanist
Manifesto in May, 1933, there was occasional talk of its

preparation. In January of that year the talk reached the project stage. The Chicago group, once it had agreed on publication, realized the difficulties of composition by committee. Unanimously it was agreed to ask Roy Wood Sellars to prepare a draft that the undertaking might be launched.

Interestingly, in the March 3, 1971, letter to Dr. Haydon, Bragg remembered it this way:

> Three of us who discussed the project had some hesitation about a committee sitting down cold to launch the matter. Better, it was thought, if someone drew up an initial draft to be maturely considered by several. . . . The certainty in me is that we wanted some one person to set down the propositions. . . .
> In the autumn of 1932, Roy Wood Sellars lectured at the University of Chicago. Afterward I talked with him at some length about the need of a formulation. I asked him if he would be willing to set things down as a starter. It was agreed that I would write him in some detail as to what several of us had in mind. That I did.

Dr. Sellars was asked and, using the foundation of his work, the collating of views and editing was begun. As time passed and with aging, Dr. Sellars began to believe that he had single-handedly produced "A Humanist Manifesto." In fact, his initial draft was the basis of much input, editing, and revision, ending with a consensus declaration.

The Draft

The authorship of "A Humanist Manifesto" has frequently been debated. As noted, Dr. Sellars is often credited. After all the editing of successive versions, enough remained of its original substance to permit Dr. Sellars to recognize himself in the document. (And most certainly Dr. Sellars was among the earliest religious liberals to use the term *humanist*, which appears in the last chapter of his book, *The Next Step in Religion*.) However, Sellars was but a principal of many minds

forming the consensus of "A Humanist Manifesto."
In a letter he wrote to me in 1970, Dr. Bragg noted:

> I saw recently, I think in the *Unitarian Universalist World*,
> that Sellars was the author of "A Humanist Manifesto."
> That, as I indicated to you during the summer, is not quite
> the case. He did the first draft and it was worked over,
> not on one occasion, as I might have indicated, but on
> several. I do wish we might get hold of that original draft
> and compare it with what was finally published. This would
> not in any way depreciate Sellars' contribution. It would,
> however, keep closer to history.

Unfortunately, the original draft may be irretrievably lost.
There were, however, nearly fifty archival drawers of material,
including dossiers on everyone prominently connected with
that new movement. In one of the drawers, we found, attached
to a vitae of Dr. Sellars listing his books through 1933 but
otherwise undated, what may be the outline of the talk Sellars
gave at the University of Chicago when Bragg first approached
him about the project—or it may be the first draft of the manifesto. We sent a copy to Dr. Sellars in 1970 asking if he could
recall which it was. Our correspondence reached him at an
Ann Arbor nursing home. At the age of ninety-one, his eyes
were weakening and he had to use a cane to get about and
could no longer care for himself. However, he claimed that
his mind was unaffected and wrote:

> I did give a talk at Chicago on invitation and it was sug-
> gested that I write something systematic and send it back
> for comments. I adopted the title "Humanist Manifesto"
> and sent the formulation back to Chicago for comment.
> There were a few separate comments on various points and
> then that second statement I took note of. This draft I sent
> out and it was sent around and signed and published.

The conviction that he had personally written and circulated "A Humanist Manifesto" appeared in correspondence
and conversations with Dr. Sellars during his advanced years
while we were seeking a copy of the original draft. On July 7,

1970, he replied from Ann Arbor:

> The point is that I wrote the Manifesto, even giving it its
> title. I have never hitherto stressed the point. But it is get-
> ting late in my career and it should be known. I think I
> wrote you that a Catholic professor at Toronto has given
> the document an author whose name I had never heard
> of. It should be settled.

On another occasion, Dr. Sellars wrote:

> I kept the first draft for a long time, even after I had retired
> and moved to Port Ryers. I remember that my son Wil-
> fred[3] sent it to me and said that I should keep it, but my
> wife Helen died, I did not think of it naturally, and it disap-
> peared. You know the old saying that a move is like a fire.

Making allowance for age and the difficulties of recol-
lecting a process that took place forty years before, we can
state with some assurance that probably Dr. Sellars was not
fully aware of the extent to which revision by others took
place. When one considers that much younger men proved
completely forgetful of the circumstances surrounding the
Humanist Fellowship and its fate—not to mention the fact their
experience with *The New Humanist* completely escaped their
memories—one can understand Dr. Sellars' foggy memory
of the considerable editing that produced the final document.

Twenty years after publication of "A Humanist Manifesto," Dr. Auer of Harvard University, a most meticulous
church historian, wrote in a letter dated March 3, 1953:

> I think you are under a misapprehension when you say that
> the Manifesto was originally written by Professor Sellars.
> I think that the first draft was originally made by Curtis
> Reese and Raymond Bragg. I recollect this because a copy
> was sent to me immediately after it had been drawn up
> and it was not a carefully written statement. Indeed, in

---

1. Professor Wilfred Sellars, also a philosopher, taught at the University of
Pittsburgh, Pennsylvania.

many points it did not resemble the present Manifesto. I recollect that Albert Dieffenbach and I worked some four or five hours over it in order to eliminate a number of inaccuracies, both historical and metaphysical. It is possible that, as the result of suggestions made by a number of people, the present Manifesto had been drawn up by Professor Sellars as the final redactor. I wonder whether you have any recollections of this?

As we shall see, both Sellars and Auer had it partly wrong. Sellars wrote the first draft, probably—according to Raymond Bragg—using as background notes from a lecture on the nature of value which he gave about that time at the University of Chicago. In the March 3, 1971, letter, Bragg wrote to Professor Haydon:

> We went over Sellars' draft on at least three successive meetings. During these meetings changes were made, and I can still see you with the draft, jotting down the agreements we reached.
>
> When we agreed that we had done with it what we wanted done, it was sent back to Sellars. I recall his response almost as if it were yesterday: "You fellows have done a good job. . . ." There is no question but what we had a draft of a manifesto prepared by Sellars. Nor is there in my mind any question that the Manifesto, as it stands, was a collective achievement. I see something of you in it. I recall that at one meeting in Chicago we argued long about a suggestion of Burtt's. Curtis, too, made contributions.

Beyond all the debate and discussion over the authorship of "A Humanist Manifesto," the point remains that Dr. Sellars contributed heavily to its formation. He was one of the steady workers for religious humanism, and a study of his book, *The Next Step in Religion*, secures in larger context his contribution to the production of the manifesto. Sellars wrote at least ten books on religion; he worked out a systematic, philosophic system of his own; and he made the ideal of *evolutionary naturalism* (the title of one of his books) central to his religious views. Moreover, in the same issue of *The New*

Humanist in which "A Humanist Manifeso" appeared, Sellars published an article interpretive of religious humanism. Two issues later, he answered criticism of the manifesto by the Reverend George R. Dodson of St. Louis.

Neither Roy Wood Sellars nor Raymond Bragg recognized the ten points outlined in the recently discovered archival document as the first draft of "A Humanist Manifesto" and so we must consider that the first draft is lost.

CHAPTER 5

The Editing Process

That there was no one writer of "A Humanist Manifesto" becomes clear as one reviews the editing process. Following the receipt of Dr. Sellars' first draft and some initial correspondence, the meetings of an editorial committee—Curtis Reese, A. Eustace Haydon, Raymond Bragg, and myself—were convened by Bragg and held in Reese's study at Abraham Lincoln Center, a social welfare agency in Chicago informally affiliated with local Unitarians and the Western Unitarian Conference.

Bragg remembered at least three meetings of the committee. As successive versions of the manifesto were developed, they were sent to out-of-Chicago collaborators so that the statement which was finally issued was a collective achievement.

An important consideration of the editing process was one of style, as shown in a letter from Haydon to Bragg dated February 2, 1933:

> How in thunder did we let that first sentence get by? It will have to be broken up or no one will get by it. As a matter of fact the whole of the first paragraph is jerky. And after all we shall be judged by a great many of these intellectuals by our ability to write clear and forceful English, *n'est ce pas?* Thanks for the copy.

A page of carefully stated editorial glosses by Dr. Haydon followed.

Others may have attended sessions of the editorial committee after its initial meeting, but records are missing and memories are vague. However, in writing "An Historical Note" about the creation of the manifesto twenty years later, Bragg recalled:

> The committee—Reese, Wilson, Haydon, Bragg—spent unnumbered hours in successive sessions culling, refining, reordering the statement. . . . The first circulation to potential signers was then prepared. The resulting correspondence was torrential. . . . The editorial task at this time emerged as a full time undertaking. While no thought was given to abandonment of the project, despite discouragement by a few honored skeptics, it was necessary to deal fairly with every thoughtful suggestion. There was consideration given to postponement until approval was closer to unanimous. The prospect was suggested that in a document involving the thought of thirty or forty or fifty minds we could expect no final, detailed formulation satisfactory to all. We could only hope for approximations, not ultimates.
>
> How many editorial sessions were held in drawing up the final draft, I do not recall. They were not few and they were lengthy. In the latter part of March the draft was mailed to about fifty individuals and each was requested to authorize the use of his signature. April 10 was the deadline.

Documentation of the correspondence is more detailed than of the editing committee's work. For sure, it is fair to state on the basis of that file of correspondence that, although not present at committee meetings, Professor J. A. C. F. Auer of Harvard University, the Reverend Albert Dieffenbach, and Professor E. A. Burtt (then of the Sage School of Philosophy at Cornell University in Ithaca, New York) were corresponding frequently with the editing committee. Obviously, all suggestions that were made could not be included.

At the editorial meetings, all present were busy taking notes, reading correspondence, and evaluating suggestions. The working manifesto was revised point by point. Subsequent drafts were then apparently dictated by Dr. Haydon and copied down by Dr. Bragg, who acted as the scribe of the meetings.

The committee decided, somewhat arbitrarily, that the May/June issue of *The New Humanist* would be a good time to publish their work. They were partly motivated by Raymond Bragg's already-planned trip east. While in New York, he could visit the religion editor for the Associated Press and attempt to get publicity for the manifesto. This target date left the planners with the month of April to obtain comments, incorporate them, and get final signatures.

Shortly after April 1, 1933, an edited copy of "A Humanist Manifesto"—specified "confidential"—was sent out with a cover letter on *New Humanist* letterhead to a limited number of people, requesting their signatures. The letter read:

> Believing that a public statement released to the press concerning the character and purpose of humanism will do much to clarify the public mind and at the same time constitute a constructive move, the enclosed Humanist Manifesto has been prepared. Among those who have worked upon it are the following: J. A. C. F. Auer, Burdette Backus, L. M. Birkhead, Raymond B. Bragg, Albert C. Dieffenbach, John H. Dietrich, A. Eustace Haydon, Curtis W. Reese, Roy Wood Sellars, and Edwin H. Wilson.
>
> The aim of the drafting committee has been to develop a statement representative of the general movement and acceptable to those whose signatures they desire. The Manifesto has been through many drafts and revisions and represents a synthesis rather than the views of any one person. Had time and clerical resources made it possible many others might appropriately have been asked to assist, but we hope that in its present form it will be signed by most of the thirty or more individuals who are being asked to sign.
>
> In requesting signatures the committee faces a further problem. For press purposes a limited list is necessary. Hence it is not now feasible to ask for the signatures of all who might appropriately be invited to support the Manifesto. Selection has been made upon the basis of published views, upon the fields or work in which such writers are active, and upon geographical location. Among those who will be asked, in addition to those mentioned above, are Harry E. Barnes, Rabbi Solomon Goldman, Max C.

Otto, John Herman Randall, Jr., Oliver L. Reiser, Maynard Shipley, Joseph Walker, F. S. C. Wicks, C. J. Keiser.

In order that this statement may be fully effective and constitute news when the signing is completed, we ask you kindly to keep the project a matter of strictest confidence until the release has appeared in the newspapers. We will welcome your comment upon the statement, particularly if you are not to appear as a signer. A blank authorizing us to use your signature is attached. Should the Manifesto meet, in general substance, with your approval, please let us have your answer no later than April 10.

Raymond Bragg signed some of these letters, and I signed the others.

Draft Text

The following draft text of "A Humanist Manifesto" was sent with the above letter. Note especially items six and fourteen, which were subjects of much continuing discussion.

(Confidential Draft)

A Humanist Manifesto

The time has come for widespread recognition of the radical changes in religious beliefs in the modern world. The time is past for mere revision of traditional attitudes. Science and economic change have disrupted the old beliefs. Religions the world over are under the necessity of coming to terms with new conditions created by a vastly increased knowledge and experience. In every field of human activity, the vital movement is now in the direction of a candid and explicit humanism. In order that religious humanism may be better understood we, the undersigned, desire to make certain affirmations which we believe the facts of our contemporary life conclusively demonstrate.

There is great danger of a final, and we believe fatal, identification of the word *religion* with doctrines and methods which have lost their significance and which are powerless to solve the problem of human living in the

Twentieth Century. Religions have always been means for realizing the highest values of life. This end has been accomplished through the interpretation of powers in nature, and the creation of a technique of worship. By means of this worship men hoped to exercise control over those powers in order to attain values considered by the group to be most desirable. A change in any of these factors results in the alteration of the outward forms of religion. This fact explains the changefulness of religions throughout the centuries. But through all changes religion itself remains constant in its quest for abiding values, an inseparable feature of human life.

Today man's larger understanding of the universe, his scientific achievements, and his deeper appreciation of brotherhood have created a situation which requires a new statement of the means and purposes of religion. Any such vital, fearless, and frank religion capable of furnishing adequate social goals and personal satisfactions may appear to many religious people as a complete break with the past. While this age does owe a vast debt to the traditional religions, it is nonetheless obvious that any religion that can hope to be a synthesizing and dynamic force for today must be created for the needs of this age. To establish such a religion is a major necessity of the present. It is a responsibility which rests upon this generation. We therefore affirm the following:

First: Religious humanists regard the universe as self-existing and not created.

Second: Humanism believes that man is a child of nature who has emerged as the result of a continuous process.

Third: Mind is a function of the organism. The traditional dualism of spirit and body must be rejected.

Fourth: Man's religious culture and civilization, as clearly depicted by anthropology and history, are the product of a gradual development due to his interaction with his natural environment and with his social heritage. The individual born into a particular culture is largely molded by that culture.

Fifth: The nature of the universe depicted by modern science makes unacceptable any supernatural or cosmic guarantees of human values. Religion must formulate its hopes and plans in the light of scientific procedure.

Sixth: We assert that the time has passed for theism, deism, modernism, and the several varieties of "new thought."

Seventh: Religion consists of those actions, purposes, and experiences which are humanly significant. Nothing human is alien to the religious. It includes labor, art, science, philosophy, love, friendship, recreation—all that is in its degree expressive of intelligently satisfying human living. The distinction between the sacred and the secular can no longer be maintained.

Eighth: Religious humanism considers the complete realization of human personality to be the end of man's life and seeks its development and fulfillment in the here and now. This is the explanation of the humanist's social passion.

Ninth: In place of the old attitudes involved in worship and prayer the humanist finds his religious emotions expressed in a heightened sense of personal life and in a cooperative effort to promote social well-being.

Tenth: It follows that there will be no uniquely religious emotions and attitudes of the kind hitherto associated with belief in the supernatural.

Eleventh: Man will learn to face the crises of life in terms of his knowledge of their naturalness and probability. Reasonable and manly attitudes will be fostered by education and supported by custom. We assume that humanism will take the path of social and mental hygiene and discourage sentimental and unreal hopes and wishful thinking.

Twelfth: Believing that religion must work increasingly for joy in living, religious humanists aim to foster the creative in man and to encourage achievements that add to the satisfactions of life.

Thirteenth: Religious humanism maintains that all associations and institutions exist for the fulfillment of human life. The intelligent evaluation, transformation, control, and direction of such associations and institutions with a view to the enhancement of human life is the purpose and program of humanism.

Fourteenth: The humanists are firmly convinced that existing acquisitive and profit-motivated society has shown itself to be inadequate and that a radical change in methods, controls, and motives must be instituted. A socialized and cooperative economic order must be established to the end that the equitable distribution of the means of life be possible. Humanists demand a shared life in a shared world.

Fifteenth and last: We assert that humanism will: (*a*) affirm life rather than deny it; (*b*) seek to elicit the possibilities of life, not flee from it; and (*c*) endeavor to establish the conditions of a satisfactory life for the many, not merely for the few. By this positive *morale* and intention humanism will be guided, and from this perspective and alignment the techniques and efforts of humanism will flow.

So stand the theses of religious humanism. Though we consider the religious forms and ideas of our fathers no longer adequate, the quest for the good life is still the central task for mankind. Man is at last becoming aware that he alone is responsible for the realization of the world of his dreams, that he has within himself the power for its achievement. He has only to set intelligence and will to the task.

During the first three weeks of April 1933, copies of "A Humanist Manifesto" were returned with approval and signatures. In spite of very limited secretarial help, it was necessary to notify as many as possible of those who had signed the draft statement of later changes. The committee and its correspondents apparently had worked on "A Humanist Manifesto" with the same meticulous pains and zeal one finds in a struggle over a social action resolution in a church assembly or on the platform of a political convention. One might compare it to the discussion over the language of policymaking legislation in some state house. The whole enterprise was undertaken with the utmost seriousness. And, as some of the responses will show, the process of consensus was not easy.

CHAPTER 6

Early Responses from Signers

Dr. E. A. Burtt

Dr. E. A. Burtt of Cornell University's Sage School of Philosophy, was one of the most prompt and thorough critics of the proposed manifesto. Six years later, in the first edition of his excellent book, *Types of Religious Philosophy*, Dr. Burtt placed religious humanism in a broad setting, comparing Bertrand Russell's humanism with that of Roy Wood Sellars' in *The Next Step in Religion*. The writings of Dr. Sellars, according to Dr. Burtt, prominently represent a more mature form of realistic humanism. Dr. Burtt contrasts Sellars' realistic humanism with pragmatic humanism.

As editing of "A Humanist Manifesto" continued, it seems that thinkers of various philosophic schools met ethically and religiously at humanism. On April 10, 1933, Dr. Burtt wrote to Raymond Bragg:

> I have just received the copy you kindly sent me of the projected Humanist Manifesto. I beg of you with all the earnestness at my command not to publish this statement without further consideration of its implications. It is not that my own agreement and signature are of any consequence, but I am sure that a manifesto in this form will distress and alienate from the humanist movement a large number of people whom it is not at all necessary to alienate. It is quite possible that this public pronouncement,

signed by the persons whose support you contemplate
securing, will mark a historic landmark in the development
of religious humanism, and will be accepted by the public
for what it claims to be, namely a creedal definition of
the essentials of religious humanism whose major implications ought to be accepted by anyone who proposes
henceforth to call himself a humanist and wishes to
cooperate fraternally in his religious life with other humanists. For this reason it seems to me that it would be a tragic
calamity not to make sure with the utmost care and caution
that the pronouncement opposes only those positions and
ideas which are irreconcilable with the essential matters
on which those in profound sympathy with the humanist
movement take their stand. Just at the moment I am ab-
sorbed in other duties that cannot be put off, but in a day
or two I shall venture to write again, making specific suggestions which in my judgment are necessary if the unfortunate consequences above mentioned are to be avoided.
Briefly, it seems to me that a natural reading of this statement would assume that it commits itself to a particular
theory of naturalism, excluding all other naturalisms such
as the Aristotelian, which would allow a certain metaphysical reality to teleological relations, irreducible to
casual connections of the material and genetic types. It
would assume that the humanism denies the reality and
religious value of all entities transcending human experience, whereas, if I have read my humanist friends correctly,
all that they mean to insist upon as essential is that if such
entities are accepted their meaning and value for us may
be constructed in terms derived solely from human experience. It would assume that humanism denies the legitimacy
of carrying over terms (such as God) from the older religious framework, whereas all that is needful to insist upon
is that if these terms are carried over they must be fully
and honestly reinterpreted in terms consistent with scientific truth and shareable human values.

Please do not make the irreparable mistake of letting
this go quite yet.

Raymond Bragg replied to Burtt on April 13, 1933:

Your letter of April 10th regarding the Humanist Manifesto

is a splendid thing. Needless to say, everyone nearest the formulation of the statement is willing to hold up publication until your suggestions are in a specific form. Indeed several exceedingly helpful and constructive suggestions have reached us since we circulated the draft. About twenty-five have signed the statement as it stands and they represent a surprising group of individuals.

I dislike to hurry you when a matter at hand is so important. However, it seems important that we get this thing in something like presentable form in the near future. When your next letter comes several of us will get together and act upon your suggestions. You are aware how difficult it is to do a thing of this sort without full conference. I undertook the general supervision of the thing and I have spent endless time on it. With limited means and a busy life it has been no easy task. I feel that it has all been profitable in view of responses both favorable and critical. I will be looking forward to hearing from you.

Dr. Burtt, however, had not waited for a reply from Bragg, because on April 12, 1933, he sent the promised additional letter. Accompanying it was the original document with the changes specified in his own handwriting. His response read:

Following my letter of yesterday I am offering herewith a few suggestions which I hope you and your friends who have been preparing the manifesto will be disposed to feel can be introduced into it without prejudice to any conviction which you and they regard as vital. If you do decide to include the substance of them I should be glad to have my name appear as one of the signers in case you wish to add it. In any event their inclusion, I believe, will aid in preventing the alienation from the humanist movement of a group of people whom there is no need to repel.

First, a few quite minor suggestions which are mainly matters of choice of words. Line 6 of second paragraph, for "exercise control over" substitute "win adjustment to." Line 3 of third paragraph, for "any such" substitute "such a." Line 8 of third paragraph, substitute "shaped" for "created." In the second thesis, for "child" substitute "part." In the fifth thesis, for "procedure" substitute "forecasts and methods." In the seventh thesis substitute the first word of the last sentence by "Any sharp." In the fifteenth thesis, end (c) with "satisfactory life for all, not merely for a few."

More important matters are, in my judgment, the following. The first sentence of the third thesis, as it stands, might seem to claim conclusiveness on a matter which science has not conclusively decided, and to commit humanism to the old-fashioned sort of materialism. Would it not be enough to say: "Mind and body are closely interconnected?" Between the fifth and sixth theses, as they stand, it would seem to me very important to insert another, reading in the substance as follows: "In denying the supernatural humanism does not deny the existence of realities transcending human experience. But it insists that the only dependable way of determining the meaning and value for us of such realities, as of any others, is by the honest study and intelligent assessment of human experiences of value realized in relation to such realities." In the same way it seems to me important to add to the sixth thesis a second sentence reading in substance: "If terms such as God, salvation, soul, and the like, are to be retained in humanist thought, they must be reinterpreted without reservation in terms of verifiable scientific knowledge and empirically discoverable human values."

The above three changes, if made, would, it seems to me, overcome the main difficulties of the manifesto in its present form. Two other additions, however, seem to me highly desirable. Since it is absurd to expect the organization of the church, the ministry, etc., to remain the same when the accompanying theology has been exploded, I should insert between the thirteenth and fourteenth theses another reading: "Humanism expects that religious associations will pass through a progressive remolding, as experience teaches the best methods by which humanists may cooperatively further their common aims." I also feel some sort of gap between the fourteenth and fifteenth theses which would be remedied by the insertion of a thesis like this: "The ultimate goal of humanism is the universal cooperation of mankind in intelligent pursuit of the common good."

I hope I have not seemed presumptuous in sending

these suggestions. The reason for my great concern is expressed in yesterday's letter, so I shall not repeat it. We may be at an important turning point in religious history, and it seems to me imperative for such a pronouncement as this to be clear and uncompromising on the fundamentals while carefully avoiding implications which are not essential to fundamentals.

John Herman Randall

On April 13, 1933, I received a letter from John Herman Randall, Jr., of the Department of Philosophy at Columbia University. Randall wrote that he had received our letter of April 10 addressed to him at Columbia but had not seen "A Humanist Manifesto" mentioned therein. In fact, he said, "I have received no copies or other communications from *The New Humanist* during the current year" and asked that his address be checked, at the same time requesting a copy of the manifesto. I replied to Professor Randall on April 7, 1933:

> I don't know by what slip a copy of the Manifesto failed to reach you. Our checklists show that a copy was sent to you in the very first batch. The Manifesto, as it stands, has received the signature of some very prominent men, including Robert Morss Lovett, John Dewey, Harry Elmer Barnes, A. J. Carlson of the Department of Physiology of Chicago University, J. A. C. F. Auer of the Harvard Divinity School, A. E. Haydon, R. W. Sellars, and over twenty others.
>
> As the Manifesto stands it it subject to some slight revisions as many constructive criticisms have come to us. Perhaps the most searching criticism received is that from Prof. E. A. Burtt of the Sage School of Philosophy at Cornell who is concerned that the manifesto shall not imply old fashioned materialism, and also not rule out certain humanists of the Aristotelian type. He suggests the following additional thesis, to be inserted between the fifth and sixth theses: "In denying the supernatural, humanism does not deny the possibility of existence of realities transcending human experience. But it insists that the only depend-

able way of determining the meaning and value to us of such realities, as of any others, is by the honest study and intelligent assessment of human experiences (of value realized in relation to such realities)."

He (Dr. Burtt) would add the following to the sixth thesis: "If terms such as God, salvation, soul, and the like are to be retained in humanist thought at all, they must be reinterpreted without reservation in terms of verifiable scientific knowledge and empirically discoverable human values."

I then summarized in my letter the suggestions made in Dr. Burtt's letter for several changes and additions in these theses.

I am giving you these suggested changes because the interested group in Chicago will have one more session to consider all suggested changes before the final release to the press, and any comment you may be able to send us by return air mail will be helpful when Bragg, Reese, Haydon, Rabbi Goldman, and myself get together this week, probably Thursday. We'd like your signature to the existing document and if any substantial changes are made we'll resubmit the Manifesto with changes to all signers. We'd like your comments on Prof. Burtt's suggestions, too. They meet the needs of men such as John Haynes Holmes and others who have been sympathetic but critical this far. We'll look forward to your answer. I am my own typist so you'll kindly excuse the form of this letter.

Although that letter mentions Rabbi Goldman, there is no record of Solomon Goldman ever having taken part in the discussion and, obviously, he never signed the manifesto.

Dr. Burtt's searching criticisms raised much concern. Dr. Randall sent us his signature on April 18, saying: "I object to Burtt's change in the third thesis, other changes acceptable. I very much dislike the crass optimism of the last two sentences of the Manifesto." And Burtt's comments prompted Dr. Bragg to write to John Dewey on April 13:

Some very constructive criticism of the form and content of the Humanist Manifesto have come to us in the last few days and have brought us to the decision that revision is advisable. Among those whose criticisms will be taken into consideration in this revision are: President Arthur E. Morgan of Antioch College, Professor E. A. Burtt of Cornell; Professor A. E. Haydon of Chicago; Dr. John Haynes Holmes.

Whether you feel able or disposed to sign the Manifesto in any form or not, we would appreciate greatly your suggestions and criticisms of the form sent to you. In case that has become lost we are sending you another copy by separate mail.

If in the next day or two you could send us your suggestions for any alterations, additions or deletions we would appreciate your advice greatly. If you wish us to withhold your name as having any connection with the Manifesto until you have had an opportunity to consider the final draft, we shall of course do so. This matter of revision changes of course the situation outlined in my letter sent to you earlier in the week.

Dr. Dewey returned the draft sent to him without change or comment—simply signing his name.

The Boston Connection

Under the leadership of Dr. Albert Dieffenbach, some of the Boston humanists consulted each other about "A Humanist Manifesto." Dr. Dieffenbach was a former editor of the Unitarian periodical, *Christian Register*[1]; a minister of the Unitarian church in Newton Center, Massachusetts; and the newly appointed religion editor of the *Boston Evening Transcript*. He wrote to Bragg on April 18, 1933, that he had had long talks with both Maynard Shipley, president and founder of the Science League of America, and Joseph Walker, a prominent

---

1. The *Christian Register* bore a name long retained by the Unitarians for the ostensible reason that it was then the oldest religious periodical in the United States to be published continuously under the same name. With the Universalist merger in 1961, the need for change prevailed, and the *Unitarian Univeralist World* became the ultimate sucessor to that denominational organ.

Boston attorney.

Maynard Shipley's fascination with science led him to publish two books: *The War on Modern Science* (1927) and *The Key to Evolution* (1929). He was a popular public and radio lecturer on astronomy and evolution. Unfortunately, Shipley died in June 1934, just thirteen months after signing the manifesto.

Joseph Walker was a good deal different from most of the manifesto's signers by virtue of his profession, his political activism, and his arrival at a humanist perspective independent of any formal movement. He had been a Republican candidate for governor of Massachusetts and, for two years, Speaker of the Massachusetts House of Representatives. In 1932, with the encouragement of John Dietrich, Walker published *Humanism As a Way of Life*. Dieffenbach wrote:

> Joseph Walker signs. He is absolutely in sympathy with our central idea, and has no use for your Millikans and Eddingtons. He will study the Manifesto and write you. He wondered if it was the right time. I told him it was, for example Auer's lectures, publications of them by the AUA [American Unitarian Association], the lining up of Dewey, Haydon, Reese, and yourself about whom he wanted "info." I told him if there was anything in the Manifesto which he might care to modify, it would be most carefully considered. On the whole, the prospect for him is good, and I hope he does not unduly delay.

Walker sent no comments, and his name was used on Dr. Dieffenbach's authority.

CHAPTER 7

Critiques from Humanists
Who Did Not Sign

Several important individuals did not sign "A Humanist Manifesto" but contributed substantially through their criticisms. The following four men are of varied backgrounds and professions and, precisely for that reason, the manifesto editors made concerted efforts to obtain their endorsements. We very much wanted the manifesto to reflect the best and broadest of humanistic thought.

Dr. Arthur E. Morgan

One of these men was Dr. Arthur E. Morgan, who is clearly in the wider stream of important nonjoining humanists by virtue of two of his books, *My World* (1927) and *Search for Purpose* (1955). His pioneer work as an engineer, his appointment as a Tennessee Valley Authority Commissioner (which led to his confrontation over policy matters with Franklin D. Roosevelt), his innovative presidency of Antioch College in Yellow Springs, Ohio, his concern for Native Americans and for small community life, and his empathy with the struggles of small communities in India all marked him as a truly great American. In his ninety-second year, he published a scholarly expose of the Army Corps of Engineers, *Dams and Other Disasters*. He was working on yet another book at the time of his death in 1975.

I had always had close ties with Dr. Morgan and Yellow Springs. In fact, in late 1949 both the publishing office of *The Humanist* and the headquarters of the American Humanist Association were moved there.

Upon receiving his confidential draft of "A Humanist Manifesto" on April 10, 1933, Dr. Morgan responded immediately in what was to become a decades-long service as an adviser to the humanist movement. Dr. Morgan wrote:

> While I agree generally with what is stated, I find my tempo unequal to the task of assimilating and appraising a new statement of a philosophy of life on a busy Saturday morning. Therefore I must forego the historic opportunity for being one of the charter members of the first universal religion.

Dr. Morgan, however, did not let the matter end there but wrote further in a letter published in its entirety in the same issue of *The New Humanist* in which "A Humanist Manifesto" first appeared:

> The hesitancy I feel about signing the Manifesto grows chiefly out of questions of emphasis rather than out of explicit disagreement. Differences as to the essence of philosophy and outlook generally originate as differences of emphasis. I believe that unless the Humanist movement achieves a better distribution of emphasis, it will act as a sectarian movement to divide those who have one partial view of the issues of life from those who have another partial view, unless by fortunate circumstance it should be displaced and eliminated by a more inclusive and adequate view.
>
> W. E. Channing, John Wesley, and George Fox each lacked something which the others could have provided. The following of each is destined to fade away, I believe, because of such lack. Had the desirable qualities of all three been united in one of them, the results might have been far more significant. George Fox, John Woolman, and others, notwithstanding untenable beliefs, had a quality of life of great necessity and value, which this manifesto may not deny but which it fails adequately to recognize. In that

respect the manifesto reflects the prevailing temper of humanists.

To touch upon another point, any vital religion must give great emphasis to faith, which in essence is an unproven conviction of the significance of living. The humanist has some of this faith, or he would have no incentive for formulating his creed.

Yet, it seems to me, humanists are not characteristically strong in faith, hope, and love. Faith is an unreasoned conviction that life is, or can be made to be, significant. The humanist temper inclines to be one of seeing justifiable faith as a sort of dispassionate statistical or scientific conclusion about things. (This may be a somewhat unfair statement.) Faith is, however, much more than that. It is a cause of things to be. What is to be is partly determined by what faith is held. The oak and the walnut grow side by side in an identical environment. As a rough analogy we might say that each becomes what it is because of its inner "faith." In the realm of the human spirit we can explore for or create vital life aims and can have faith that such a pursuit is of great significance. It is the function of intelligence to enlighten faith and to protect it from error, but not to clip its wings, and not to compel it to walk because intelligence cannot fly.

Hope is the drive and expectation with which faith is held. To a large degree it determines how great shall be the results. Some time ago I heard a prominent humanist talking to college students. I thought what a pity for them to be under the influence of a man who expects so little from life. He seemed like one whistling to keep up his courage through a graveyeard or on the way to the gallows. Very rarely will men's lives outrun their hopes, and rarely are their hopes untouched by the quality of their lives.

Love is all that Paul said it is. If it is not strong, all else is weak. I feel this very keenly in my own case. For the past twelve years I have been associated with a rare lot of young people. So far as a native quality is concerned they would have supplied a dozen groups of twelve apostles, every one better than the best of the historic twelve. We have had the raw material to turn America to a new course, but it has gone through our institution and has passed on, sometimes much better for the experience, and sometimes disillusioned and bewildered.

Faith, hope, and love are usually transmitted by contagion from persons who possess those qualities, but the human associations which transmit them generally have transmitted also an uncritical credulity. Those who are free from that uncritical credulity commonly are also free to a considerable extent from the faith, the hope, and the warm love of men which so commonly accompanied that credulity in our religious history, when nearly all men were credulous. The same environmental causes probably led to the absence of credulity and the absence of the desirable qualities. We might also say that such was the price of intellectual freedom. We have not yet learned to separate our cultural inheritance into its elements and to select and reject with sincerity and with critical intelligence.

The spiritual lassitude and disillusionment of many young people are partly due to the fact that they have been introduced into a critical atmosphere without having been equipped or indoctrinated in early childhood with spiritual drives and enthusiasms to carry them through such a crisis. Sometimes they lack sensitiveness to aspiration because that sensitiveness was not instilled early. Yet as I have considered the causes of this large degree of failure on my part I believe it is not due primarily to intellectual limitations or to lack of hard work, but that its cause may be illustrated by Paul's phrase—"Though I give my body to be burned, and have not love, it profiteth me nothing" [1 Corinthians 13:3].

I think it was primarily that quality of love for men which gave Abraham Lincoln his orientation and his power. It is that quality which has given him his dominant place in history. . . .

Orthodox people will say that the lack of strong development of these qualities is evidence of fundamental unsoundness of humanism. I do not agree with that attitude. Our patterns of life are usually taken bodily from our environment or from some parts of it. The same pattern, which in the past included faith, hope, and love, commonly also included an uncritical and traditional attitude toward life, since such uncritical attitude was common to mankind.

I believe this association of elements was a historical accident, and was not an essential connection. The following is an example of the accidental historical association of qualities that have no inherently necessary relation:

For a long time I have searched for a man to head up a small industry. It was necessary that he have sound and discriminating and well-tested judgment in business matters, and that he have discipline of character to act with decision and with forethought. It was also necessary that he should not be controlled by the prevailing profit motive or by self-interest, and that he should not measure his success by his financial income.

Such people, I find to be relatively few. The reason, I believe, is that since business in general is controlled by the profit motive and recognizes self-interest as dominant, any person who serves an apprenticeship to business, which is about the only way to develop business skill and judgment, by that same apprenticeship becomes indoctrinated with the profit motive and with self-interest, since they are so nearly always present. Because of this historical association, it is relatively common to find keen and able business men whose business conduct is dominated by self-interest, or to find altruistic and self-forgetting persons who are incompetent in business, but relatively uncommon to find business keenness and acumen combined with altruism and self-forgetfulness. Could we once get started a race of business men who would consider business primarily as a public trust, and who would take out only enough income to make them effective in their work, then the new combination would be just as natural as the old.

The draft of a humanist manifesto exposes this condition. As I said before, it is a matter of emphasis, not one of intellectual approval or disapproval. I doubt whether I can suggest a thesis in addition to meet this weakness. The quality must be implicit in the movement in order to have adequate expression in a manifesto, though it is well to do the best possible for its inclusion.

The problem of humanism is to do that—to hold faithfully to a completely open-minded and critical attitude, while holding to, or eagerly seeking, the strong drives of faith, hope, and love. As such strong drives appear they will express themselves in heroic living, and by contagion will be transmitted.

Your fifth item reads in part: "The nature of the universe depicted by modern science makes unacceptable any supernatural or cosmic guarantees of human values." After eliminating the words "supernatural or", it is still a theoretical negation of this faith, not by what it says, but by what it leaves unsaid. That statement has an unjustified cocksureness, and is not dictated by humility or imagination. Religion must be disciplined by scientific procedure, but not limited to it, except as a poet or musician should be so limited. It must run far ahead of a science.

Religion should instill a hot partisanship for life which shall set for science the task of finding significance or of creating it. "Wishful thinking", if wisely inspired, may cause the discovery or creation of the values wished for. Our business is to find significance, or to create it. Lest we miss the real possibilities, this attitude drives us to the most relentless criticisms and the most ruthless testing of assumptions. Lacking that faith, we will not take the trouble to search and test, and so may miss the greatest realities. Your manifesto fails adequately to recognize the source of your own driving power.

When young people without a religious background become indoctrinated with such a creed as you present, they discern the inconsistency between the concern you express for social progress and the lack of inclusive significance for life as a whole. With reference to a great discipline of life or to immediate social effort they will say, "What's the use." They may have little appetite for living. I am not speaking in the abstract, but from observation of students who have shown just such development from just such causes. If there are great and undiscovered possibilities for life, their disillusionment and lack of drive would destroy incentive and leave those values undiscovered.

Another point—the repeated insertion of "human" before "life" implies that only in the species *Homo sapiens* can there be significance.

When I criticize the humanists in general I criticize myself, for some of their typical weaknesses are my own. If what I say is to be of any value I must speak plainly and perhaps not without offense. A movement like humanism is determined not solely or primarily by a statement of policy but also by the types of the personalities that lead it.

These are some of the reasons why I hesitate to have

my position defined by this manifesto. The statement shows great progress, and I admire and approve its courage.

Although Dr. Morgan never joined the American Humanist Association, he continued to be in touch with it throughout his career. He was actively involved in securing a minister for the Unitarian Church of Dayton, Ohio, and was once the moderator of the American Unitarian Association; however, at some point, he dropped out of Unitarianism and announced that his sole label would be that of the Society of Friends, his wife Lucy's church. The Yellow Springs Meeting of the Quakers, to which he belonged, was the most humanistic of all the Quaker circles I have ever encountered.

I used to see Dr. Morgan quite frequently, and once he remarked to me: "Humanism's all right; it's the humanists!" Through Antioch College and its students, the wisdom of this seasoned educator has inspired and nourished the culture of many decades.

John Haynes Holmes

John Haynes Holmes, minister of the Community Church of New York, provided valuable criticism which the manifesto editors took under careful consideration. In 1927, Holmes had contributed to *Humanist Sermons*, edited by Curtis Reese. Throughout his career, Holmes was renowned for the eloquence of his public speaking.

At the time we were publishing "A Humanist Manifesto," he was the editor-in-chief and Curtis Reese was the associate editor of *Unity*, a periodical published by the Western Unitarian Conference in Chicago. It is important to distinguish this publication from another by the same name, published in Kansas City; the latter had as its general theme that "as a man thinketh so is he, so think fondly sweet thoughts." In general, religious liberals and the editors of the Chicago *Unity* found the Kansas City publication saccharine but less harmful than *Christian Science*.

Holmes eventually withdrew from the editorial board of

Unity, as he and Reese differed seriously on a number of issues, including pacifism during World War II. Holmes' theism and views on immortality hardly put him in the humanist ranks, although his pacifism and forthrightness on civil liberties made him a lasting hero of socially relevant religion. Holmes stated in his initial response to Bragg regarding the manifesto:

I have been studying with the utmost care the Manifesto which you are preparing to publish, for I count myself a humanist in the broader and more inclusive sense of the word.

Nearly every one of the items of your program is satisfactory to me, although I might desire to change the wording here and there. But there is one exception—the Sixth. I do not feel, and certainly do not want to assert, [that] "the time has passed for theism"! I have never at any time seen any necessary contradiction between humanism on the one hand and theism on the other. Indeed, I believe that a true humanism inevitably unfolds into a rational theism, or may at least be consistent therewith. Theism is to my mind the blossom which grows upon the plant of humanism, the poetry into which it unfolds in mystic beauty. As I look at it, God is only another word for Humanity, as America is only another word for the United States.

You speak of deism! Well, now, deism isn't half bad! As a precise type of philosophical and theological thought it is, of course, old-fashioned and terribly unscientific, but it has a fundamental poetic value. After all, there is a religion of nature—see Wordsworth—and deism was a crude attempt to explain it, if you know what I mean. At bottom, I don't see why, in a modern Manifesto, the word "deism" should appear at all, as it belongs to the eighteenth century. You wouldn't refer in this statement to Platonism, positivism, or monism—why bother with deism?

As for modernism, I think this is a terribly loose word. Who knows what you mean? Why isn't humanism to be regarded as modernism of the best type? Modernism to my mind depends on the modernist—that is, upon the man who holds it—and I would not deny the term as applied either to you or to me. The word has no definite content at all, and therefore to my mind should not be used.

What I am objecting to at bottom is the whole spirit of this Sixth Thesis. You are arbitrarily ruling out from our thought something about which you know absolutely nothing at all. You are insisting, or at least suggesting, that in some way, traditional or otherwise, there is a fundamental contradiction between humanism and theism. I deny this! I insist that they are complementary. From one point of view at least, I would describe humanism as the right road to theism. Whether you and I, in traveling this road, will ever arrive at our goal is a question. It may be a question as to whether the road has ever been broken through to the goal. You have perhaps traveled as far as the road can take you, and I am insisting on going on and losing myself in the unexplored landscape. What you are trying to say in your Manifesto, or the most of what you are trying to say, is that the humanist road, as far as it goes, is the only road a sound thinker can travel. And I deny that you have any right to say that the road ends at the point where you stop your journey and that nothing lies beyond.

Thus John Haynes Holmes took the manifesto seriously but, in the end, could not sign it. On April 13, 1933, he wrote to Raymond B. Bragg:

Thanks for your letter of the 12th. Let me say how much it pleases me that you really want me to join your good company of signers of the Humanist Manifesto. I certainly want to sign, but I am still troubled in my mind.

I think that the change you propose in the Thesis to which I objected is an improvement, but I doubt if it meets the real difficulty I have in mind. It may perhaps, in its actual thought as resident in your mind, but not, I think, in its form of statement, which might very well convey very different ideas to other minds. . . .

As for theism, putting the adjective "traditional" before it helps some, but not much. You see, I have a great respect for theism. It may be a hangover from my early training, but it represents to me something real and true. At bottom, I don't think you can interpret the universe in terms of little, atomic, vermin-like creatures who swarm upon this infinitesimally insignificant planet of ours. We have got to begin our interpretation with these silly creatures, as we are such creatures ourselves, and therefore must start with what we know or imagine about ourselves. But to insist that we shall measure the cosmos by the limitations of our experience is to me ridiculous. I think we've got to leap beyond ourselves, use the vision or imagination or faith that the scientists use, and when we do this in theology, we call the attempt, or the result, theism. Of course, the content of theism is pretty fantastic and I suppose basically unreal, but I insist that it isn't a bit more fantastic or unreal than what the scientists are giving us these days in their quantum theories and all the rest. In other words, in using this word, "theism," traditional or otherwise, and casting it out into utter darkness, I think you are doing as arrogant and fundamentally as ignorant a thing as any dogmatist who ever lived.

I feel that I should be hopelessly misunderstood if I signed your Manifesto with this Sixth item reading in this way, I have got to say that I cannot sign up.

I fear that this is a terribly bungling statement, but it is the best I can do "right off the bat." If I must be excommunicated, I shall quite understand and love you just the same. For after all, it is your Manifesto, and not mine.

Recognizing that the criticisms of Holmes and others, coming at this late hour, were so drastic that to publish anything would require a complete halt of the proposal, Bragg wrote to Holmes on April 18, 1933:

We are going ahead with the Humanist Manifesto in a little different form though not different content. I wonder if you would permit us to publish some of your criticism contained in your letter to me in *The New Humanist* for May-June. We want to show other sides of the matter and your permission in this matter will help much.

The editors received Holmes' permission and reprinted his letter in *The New Humanist* along with "A Humanist Manifesto."

Exactly how "humanist" Holmes was is a matter of debate. I once heard an Ohio University professor, addressing the Unitarian Universalist Fellowship in Athens, Ohio, give a devastating refutation of immortality, using point by point a sermon by John Haynes Holmes on that topic. However, Carl Hermann Voss, in *Rabbi and Minister: The Friendship of Stephen S. Wise and John Haynes Holmes*, reveals clearly that Holmes held faith in immortality, God, and puritanism. Obviously, Holmes was not the type of naturalistic humanist found among the signers of "A Humanist Manifesto."

But still, Holmes was an outstanding champion of the social gospel of his day. And on social issues, in opposition to war, and in concern for the poor and outcast, he as well as most humanists were going in the same direction—and still are.

Cassius J. Keyser

Another gentleman we actively pursued for his signature on the manifesto was Dr. Cassius J. Keyser, a mathematician at Columbia University from 1897 to 1927, at which time he became professor emeritus of mathematics. On April 10, 1933, I wrote to Dr. Keyser:

> I am writing to let you know that we are delaying the release of the Humanist Manifesto until a few more of the signatures come in. We are disappointed not to have received your signature to date. If you have not sent it by the time this letter reaches and can do so will you kindly send us your signature at once either by wire or by air mail? For your information, we have had very encouraging response. Among the signers are Robert Morss Lovett, editor of *The New Republic*, Maynard Shipley, president of the Science League of America, Llewellyn Jones, literary critic, Harry Elmer Barnes, and Roy Wood Sellars. . . . We shall continue to hope for your early reply.

Professor Keyser penciled on this letter a simple remark: "I am unable to sign the Manifesto although I am in hearty accord with much of it."

Bragg followed up with a letter dated April 14, asking whether Keyser would take the time to offer specific comments on the document and his differences with it as it stood. He told Dr. Keyser:

> We want to revise this thing still further. We want it as representative as possible. If you can possibly spare the time, won't you jot down whatever feeling you may have about the form and the various points? We would like to have your reply as soon as possible.

Again, Keyser wrote on the note: "I seem to have lost my copy of the Manifesto so I am unable to comment upon its terms."

I think this exchange of letters illustrates how carefully the editors were attempting to elicit suggestions and criticisms in order to produce a document that was truly a reflection of the best thought in the movement.

Harlow Shapley

An astronomer at the Harvard College Observatory, Harlow Shapley was another who received the confidential statement and request for signature, but he, too, declined. After having sent him a personal letter, Bragg wrote to him again on April 15, 1933:

> I am enclosing a more formal letter that was sent to a number of individuals representing a scientific naturalism in one way or another. The letter, I believe, outlines what some of us had in mind when we drew up this general statement. We would be very glad to have your signature if you feel interested enough to lend your support to the statement.
>
> It has already been signed by John Dewey, Maynard Shipley, Oliver Reiser, A. J. Carlson of Chicago, Roy Sellars of Michigan, and others. Prof. Auer of the Divinity School at Harvard has been part of the effort, as you will see.
>
> It would be good to have a word from you in the near future. At all events won't you comment on the general propositions? We would like your feeling about it all.

Dr. Shapley's reply, dated April 21, 1933, expresses the reticence of some scientists to speak outside their field and chides those who use their authority as scientists to speak out on religion:

I have from time to time in the past week considered the communications sent by you and the invitation to join in the Humanist Manifesto.

As a social philosopher I am embryonic and I have decided that I should not misuse my position by pretending to intelligence or comprehension in a field in which my thoughts have been too scattered and probably too prejudiced.

The recent spectacle of one highly trained successful scientist after another becoming soft and religiously traditional has been very painful to many of us. We find it hard to live down the softer moments of Milliken, Eddington, and others.

Personally I have not yet convinced myself that current civilization which systematically protects the weak *is* in keeping with the biological traditions of the planet. I assume, but it has not been proved to me, that such elementary habits as kindness are justifiable in a close analysis.

I ask myself if we are as yet psychologically and biologically far enough from the jungle to replace emotional religion for the masses by cold and more rational philosophy.

The Manifesto is beautifully expressed, and the principles announced are inspiring. I subscribe almost in toto. But I wonder if we are ready for a religion of intelligence; and if so is it spontaneous enough, when nurtured by a deliberate manifesto?

Is the word *religion* correctly used in the Manifesto? Your affirmation numbered Seventh defines it so broadly that I suggest the word *life* or *activity* as equally appropriate.

Personally I feel that I should keep clear, knowing my ignorance, from any movement to which the word religion can be attached openly. I try to be a scientist. Science is chiefly a matter of the intelligence; religion is chiefly a matter of the emotions.

We understand stars better than we do the planets or animals because the stars are gaseous and there are fewer degrees of freedom and simpler laws. Religions and philosophies are just as much more complicated than animals as animals are more complicated than stars. A new humanism is a compact of so many variables and unknown parameters that nothing can be predicted; and this humanism is still more inexpressible in equations.

I mean by the preceding paragraphs that I feel that my sphere of activity should remain in the attempted interpretation of stars, nebulae, galaxies, and expanding universes—relatively simple enterprise—and that I should not venture at this stage of my activity into the complicated neuroses which we call civilization. I admit that the difficult phrase "fulfillment of human life" entices me as a personal and social dogma but I do not know what it means. I am sorry that I am so useless to you.

I find it interesting that later, in his retirement years, Harlow Shapley became actively interested in exploring the relationship of science and religion, cooperating with Ralph Burhoe, editor of *Zygon—Journal of Religion and Science.* Although Dr. Burhoe and the magazine (later edited by Dr. Karl Peters of Rollins College) received considerable acclaim, I was never convinced that Burhoe's effort was more than a sophisticated form of theistic apologetics.

CHAPTER 8

Unitarian Humanists Who Feared a Creed

Some of the men who declined to sign "A Humanist" Manifesto" were active writers in the humanist movement before and after the publication of the document. Four of them were Unitarian in background and affiliation, and, of them, two were published in the same issue of *The New Humanist* in which the manifesto appeared.

While the manifesto framers were careful to disclaim the document as a creed, it has nonetheless been interpreted as such. Among Unitarians, there is a historical tendency to be skeptical of creeds. Max C. Otto, Harold Buschman, James H. Hart, and E. Stanton Hodgin, in keeping with this tradition of skepticism, abstained from signing the manifesto.

Max C. Otto

Prior to 1933, Max Otto (professor of philosophy), Horace M. Kallen, and V. T. Thayer (a signer of the manifesto) were all young men on the faculty at the University of Wisconsin at Madison. V. T. Thayer was an educator and editor who wrote extensively on church-state separation. At one time, Max Otto and Horace Kallen roomed with the Thayers. According to Dr. Thayer, there was an occasion when the three young men were the lone dissenters on an issue before the campus. This position would not be unusual for anyone whose thinking was generally categorized as radical, as was the case with this group.

(Unfortunately, the manifesto editors did not contact Dr. Kallen in 1933 to seek his signature and advice. However, because he was continuously important to humanism, I have included him in this history. When asked in 1973 why he had not been invited to sign "A Humanist Manifesto" in 1933, Kallen wrote to me that John Dewey had once asked him to sign the document. He explained that he had responded to Dewey by saying that he had had stronger objections (left unspecified) to signing the 1933 document than "Humanist Manifesto II" in 1973.)

Max Carl Otto, although he declined to sign "A Humanist Manifesto," never wavered in his humanism and was the author of a series of important books and reference material on church-state and educational issues. In response to the request for his signature on the manifesto, Dr. Otto replied on April 4, 1933:

> I cannot believe that publishing the "Humanist Manifesto" will in the slightest degree "clarify the public mind" or "constitute a constructive work" in any significant sense. It will, on the contrary, I fear, be one of those theoretical gestures which leave with some persons a feeling that something has really been done when all that has been done is that something has been said. I am of the opinion that Humanism, as I understand the philosophy of it, cannot be "sold" to men and women; it must be attained by them, and that means slow, painstaking work. Much as I regret to say, No, to your request that I join you in a general announcement of ideas and aims, I do so with real conviction. Why must we, too, advertise?

We published his subsequently amplified comments in the same issue of *The New Humanist* in which the manifesto appeared:

> Publication of the "Humanist Manifesto" will, in my opinion, serve no sufficient purpose. I cannot believe with you that it will clarify the public mind, or do constructive work for the cause. A set of fifteen principles, detached from

the living experience which precipitated them and lacking the life and warmth of the interests they represent, can do little to inform the mind and nothing to stir the heart. Humanism—if I understand the philosophy of it—cannot be "sold" to people. If the "Manifesto" were a rallying cry issuing with glowing conviction from a group on the march together, or if it gave promise of gripping men and women of humanistic leanings, drawing them into closer, more understanding and more active unity, it would be a desirable signal. Unfortunately, I see no such service in it. And experience has taught me to beware of deceiving myself into thinking something has really been done when all that has been done is that something has been said. It would be easier for me to write, "Sure, go ahead, put me down." If I take the harder course and do not sign the document which I know will carry the names of men I greatly admire and respect, it is because of a deep conviction that the "Manifesto" will prove to be an ineffectual gesture, and a tactical error.

It is not surprising that Otto refused to sign, given his view on humanism. In his 1949 book, *Science and the Moral Law*, he said: "All Humanisms have one thing in common. It is the ideal of realizing man's completist development. From here on they diverge."

Harold Buschman

Harold Buschman, who played an important role in the development of humanism as the editor of *The New Humanist*, also abstained from signing the manifesto because of his fear of creeds. By 1933, Buschman had moved to New York City, where he was associated with the Ethical Culture movement with a view toward becoming an ethical leader (the equivalent of a minister).

Certainly Buschman did not impede the publishing of the manifesto, but he was highly dubious of it. Much of his apprehension was based upon his fear that the document would become a creed. Buschman, Bragg, and I were all graduates of the Meadville Theological School. However,

Buschman was never ordained a minister, nor did he become an ethical leader. He was a scholar but not an orator.

The New Humanist reprinted most of Buschman's letter of April 17, 1933:

> Any creed excludes and this is no exception. I find myself so essentially akin to individual humanists with regard to much that is regarded as important by "Humanism" that I deplore the effect of the manifestos. It serves to accentuate differences. I personally do not mind that. I can only say then, "If this is Humanism, I am not a humanist," because this creed does not approximate my individual construction of my experience. I simply do not recognize myself in this manifesto. What I deplore is the differences, the exclusions so occasioned will surely be no more profitable than previous ones. There will be "heresies" and misunderstandings instead of a free checking of experiences, one with another, without this business of sectarianism getting into our way. It may be that liberalism is doomed on every front including this one. Very well—if this is so, then I shall set out to find a sect, political rather than religious, where I shall be able to adhere to a program and a doctrine which is really pointed and not amorphous, and which is more dynamic and more related to the affairs of the day than the present document. I am not yet convinced that the doom of liberalism is sealed. Until I am, let me refrain from signing the manifesto.

James H. Hart

The third Unitarian abstainer, and one whose correspondence is missing from the archives, is the Reverend James H. Hart. Before moving to New York, Hart was minister of the Unitarian Church at Madison, Wisconsin. He and I attended Dr. Haydon's classes at the University of Chicago.

Hart contributed to *Humanist Sermons* (edited by Curtis Reese) and was, by this time, as was Harold Buschman, associated with the American Ethical Union. In the humanist archives, there is a box of his Unitarian sermons from Madison (and elsewhere). A careful worker and close friend of

Otto, most of Hart's sermons were so prophetic that even now they seem almost contemporary. He wrote so well so consistently that he rarely needed editing.

In two superb articles in *The New Humanist*, Hart showed an awareness of "the curse of bigness," anticipating *The Lonely Crowd* by many years. In the March/April 1932 issue of *The New Humanist*, in an article entitled "The Lost Individual," he wrote:

> . . . one of the characteristics of our civilization is the number of us who feel homeless and lost. . . . There is little left, indeed, that we can measure or steer by. There are no stars by which we might plot a course. . . .

His sense of the tragic can be felt here. However, as a socially conscious humanist, he looks to the repatterning of the world:

> The pathfinders shall arise from among the artists and thinkers, the managers and workers, the really germinal minds and professions. And not from among any one group of them. But from a wide cooperation, a pooling of knowledge, insight and power, towards which all groups contribute and in which they all share. . . . When we have established a society built after this fairer pattern, the Lost Individual may find himself at home again.

Added to Hart's awareness of the tragic in life and his vision of a shared world with the intelligence, good will, and skill needed to achieve it, he reveals existentialist sensitivity long before the existential movement made its impact on modern thought. In the January/February 1933 issue of *The New Humanist*, he wrote an article called "A Religious Mood," in which he said:

> The sufferer walks alone in a harsh, bitter land; and there is no help for him in the thought of science, or the almost miraculous powers that have come into man's hand. They cannot enter this region, much less bring it under control. He remembers the chants sung in their praises as one remembers trivial things, and faraway days that are scarcely a memory for him. No doubt man has won many victories

of which he may well sing with pride, but such pride seems vain and empty when love meets death and yet cannot die.

The sense of mortality is the most sombre of the elements that mingle in a religious mood. But it is only one of them and must not be magified out of proportion. And now that I have set it among the others, I need mention no more. For the mood is more than its elements, even though one were to mention them all. It refuses to be translated into anything other than itself. When that attempt ceases, it remains what it was before such translation began —a unique, living experience, a deep, gathered response of the spirit to the destiny within which it moves.

In response to our request for his signature to the manifesto, Hart wrote to Bragg in early April:

Your "theses" arrived too late for me to append my signature by the 10th. So far I have had no time to think over the statement of belief. But I find myself a bit perturbed lest we should drift into another dogmatism.

Some of the statements (a mere cursory reading) challenge one. Why must humanists go on record about "continuous processes" or stand by a certain doctrine of "Mind"? Must humanists swear by Haydon & Sellars? And science—well, the *nature* of science needs to be clearly set out before I'm ready to move.

Once again, religion appears to be so broad a thing from the statement as to be nothing. I'm inclined to believe that Religion & Ethics need disentangling.

As for any social program—concrete and provoking— I don't find anything but mere words. The other churches have at least gone on record concerning some things.

It appears to me that some of the "academic" humanists are still verbalizing mainly & don't seem to realize that much water has gone under the bridges of our common existence since the war. But I'll try to study the statement, as I have leisure.

Apparently the leisure never came, for we did not hear from him again. But as with Buschman and many other Unitarian-trained men, I suspect that the fear of a creed or dogma remained the dominant, though not the only factor, in his abstention.

Bragg replied to Hart on April 15, 1933:

> I am glad to have your letter about the proposed statement.
> I agree in many ways with you. But it is a devilish job to
> give form to a statement that will represent a number of
> individuals. The replies thus far have been interesting. Otto
> wrote as you and I would expect him to. John Dewey
> without comment appended his signature even without the
> elimination of a comma or the insertion of a period. Robert
> Morss Lovett wrote a rather enthusiastic note. Arthur
> Morgan was pleasant but doubtful. John Haynes Holmes
> has written two letters, the second more perplexing than
> the first. At one point he said that he supposes the para-
> phernalia of theism is queer. But none the less he is rather
> fond of it. Burtt wrote a corking good letter in critical vein.
> Now I feel a little less sure about the present form. But
> with the signatures we have it will be a little difficult to
> retrace our steps.

Hart's most telling criticisms of humanism were forth-
coming after publication of the manifesto and were based on
the elements he expressed in his earlier articles—the sense
of the tragic, human pride, the worth and uniqueness and even
the helplessness of human beings confronted with "forces
beyond either their understanding or control, and struggling
with enemies they can neither conquer nor leave alone." Hart
showed that a need for spirituality within a nonsupernatural
framework can be incorporated with naturalistic humanism
and broadens and deepens its dimensions on the experiential
side. Asked about Hart's experience with the American Ethical Union, V. T. Thayer wrote:

> Hart's first experiences in the [New York Ethical] Society
> were deeply disappointing and I think he suffered deeply.
> Felix Adler failed to appreciate his fine qualities and Hart,
> in turn, was badly hurt by Adler's treatment of him and
> could find little in Adler's philosophy with which he could
> agree. For a brief period, as a salvage operation, Hart taught
> a history class at Fieldston, but only for a short time, less
> than a year, I recall. He abandoned plans he had when

he came to New York to occupy the Sunday platform of the Society. He assisted George O'Dell, editor of the *Standard* [a publication of the American Ethical Union], for a period and served as a research assistant to Dr. Elliott after Adler's death. Dr. Elliott fully appreciated Hart's abilities and was very fond of him. Hart's finest hours in New York were when he assumed charge of the many programs and activities of the Society designed to help the refugees from Germany and Austria find a place in and adjust to American life. In this connection, he performed a truly remarkable job.

E. Stanton Hodgin

The fourth Unitarian minister who declined to sign the manifesto was E. Stanton Hodgin, then at First Congregational Society Unitarian Church at New Bedford, Massachusetts. Hodgin was a worthy successor to religious radical William J. Potter, who had been minister of the society for more than thirty years and was a true humanist forerunner before the word *humanist* was in use in Unitarianism.

On April 18, 1933, he replied to Bragg's request for his signature to the manifesto:

> I received your communication some time ago and read the "manifesto" with much interest. I think it is quite as well for all concerned that my name be not attached to it. I am not much of a crusader and I have found that I could preach my views, whether humanist or socialist, more effectively if I use no classifications and wear no labels. We need crusaders on the fireing [*sic*] line and we also need workers within the ranks, and it is for each to find where he can do his work most effectively.

Later on, in 1948, while in a Unitarian retirement home in Los Angeles, Hodgin wrote his views in *Confessions of an Agnostic Clergyman*. He avoided labeling himself a humanist but indicated that, over the course of a forty-year ministry, he had been on the naturalistic and humanistic side of theological issues. On page 201 of his book, Hodgin writes:

During the latter half of the nineteenth century there were in every community a number of aggressively anti-church people who accepted Robert G. Ingersoll as their leader. They were rough and ready, hard-boiled and argumentative, with keener minds and more modern knowledge than the church groups. They were usually active in reform and humanitarian movements in the communities in which they lived. It is difficult to understand now how widespread Ingersoll's influence was in those days. The Unitarians, so far as this group and the revivalistic Christians were concerned, were between the devil and the deep sea. They were not Christian enough to go with the orthodox, and they were not anti-Christian enough for the agnostics. Some of the Ingersollians toned down and made good Unitarian church members, but for the most part they were too intensely individual to fit into any organization.

This paragraph, I believe, aptly characterizes Hodgin and demonstrates his "label-phobia"; *agnostic* seems to have been sufficient for Hodgin.

CHAPTER 9

Style and Semantics

It is my contention that those who signed "A Humanist Manifesto" in 1933 sought verbal integrity and a semantic change from traditional religious terms in order to clarify their naturalistic approach. However, as is the case with most editorial matters, a great deal of the response to the written word is subjective. Needless to say, there were critics of the style and semantics of the original draft.

Among those who voiced such objections—and perhaps one of the most critical—was Dr. Bruce Swift, then minister of the Universalist church in Buffalo, New York. One must appreciate, however, that Dr. Swift was unaware of the involved process by which the statement was being produced as a reflection and reconciliation of varied viewpoints by the editors, who were working under the pressure of a deadline. Dr. Swift thought his suggested revisions included a needed literary style; I disagree. On April 6, 1933, Swift wrote to Dr. Raymond Bragg:

> Thank you for sending me a copy of the Humanist Manifesto. I went over it carefully three or four times with the result that I felt more strongly each time that some of the statements were unnecessarily hazy. If it is for public consumption then the public needs to be considered—and especially that part of it which will not read very far in a document that is not very clear. Again, I wondered at the

lack of form and still further at the complete ignoring of literary values. If this statement is likely to become a historic document why should it not be given a better form that [*sic*] it has, yea, the best form it can have?

I, therefore, do not wish my name to appear on a document which does not reflect in any adequate measure the ability of the men who drew it, that has too many earmarks of haste.

To make all this clear I have taken the time out of a busy day to re-write the thing. I do not expect this draft to be substituted for yours. It was easier, I found after writing a page of comment and criticism, to lay it aside and to re-write the document itself. I am sending this "re-write" to you as my comment. It is a first draft and can be mightily improved. I do not send it as an example; I send it as an illustration—a commentary in the form of a paraphrase.

You will see that I have omitted point FIFTEEN as a point; it is a summary pointing to a conclusion.

I do hope the document given to the press is a more carefully prepared statement than the one you sent me. Humanists claim to have THOUGHT, and they have, but *relly* [*sic*] this document does not flatter any of the men who have produced it. I am sorry to have to be so brutally frank about it but I should hate to see Humanism set forth in any but the clearest terms and best form.

In 1973, we inquired of Clinton Lee Scott as to what had happened to Dr. Swift. Scott, the 1963 recipient of the American Humanist Association's Humanist Pioneer Award and superintendent of the Universalist Churches of New England, was always outspoken in his humanist views. He wrote back:

Bruce Swift came to the Universalists I think from Presbyterian background, and became minister of the church in Buffalo in 1927 where he stayed for 10 or 11 years, then went to the Parkside Presbyterian Church, a wealthy congregation. St. Lawrence gave him a DD in 1932.

Swift was older than I, so he must be dead and gone to a Presbyterian heaven.

One can imagine what a difficult editorial problem would have confronted the committee if all of those to whom the confidential draft had been sent had, like Swift, presented *en toto* their own preferred statements. Consensus is not reached that way.

Spurred by criticisms of style, including those of Bruce Swift, the editors decided to seek expert help. In the later editing, we inserted a statement to the effect that we should not use words for which there was no verifiable referent.

Still, the question of style continued to be at issue. One such controversy arose over the use of the semantic plank. Philosopher E. A. Burtt suggested using it; Professor Robert Morss Lovett suggested dropping it. Dr. Bragg wrote of Burtt's suggestion in an April 18 letter to Dr. Lovett:

> I am enclosing a copy of a revised draft of a Humanist Manifesto. The changes are not in substance, or only slightly so, but in form. Edwin Burtt made one or two helpful suggestions and they have been included.
>
> Could you find time in the next day or two to go over the thing, checking it for the last time. Some of us have been so close to the job for weeks that we are getting stale. Your word on punctuation, construction, etc., would ease our minds. We seem to have done about everything we are capable of.
>
> It ought not to take a great deal of time. We are eager to release it in the near future. You will be interested to see the list of signatures. John Dewey, Harry Barnes, Burtt have gone along with us. It would not be surprising if we caused some turmoil in the religious press. Let us hope!

Dr. Lovett, however, suggested dropping the semantic plank. On April 20 he replied:

> I have looked over the Humanist Manifesto and made no changes, except scattering a few commas. Except in article 6, I think it rather absurd to instruct people as to how they shall use certain words. These words have a metaphorical value in literature, and I should say it was impossible to use them to symbolize "verifiable scientific knowledge," etc. I think this sentence unfortunately naive, and tending

to color the whole document. It will certainly be seized upon for destructive comment. Personally, I cannot give up God in such expressions as "God damn it all!" any more than I can give up liquor.

I resent the *must* in both cases.

Bragg replied briefly:

I think your suggestion on the Sixth Thesis all to the good. Burtt was responsible for that revision and it went in with only the half hearted support of the drafting committee. I am glad you checked us in such round terms.

So, the semantic clause was dropped, leaving a loophole for the use of theistic language. Dr. Lovett's remark has always caused me to wonder if profanity is the point of ultimate survival for "God language."

Bragg then wrote to Burtt on April 21:

In line with the suggestions you made in your recent letter to me the content of the Humanist Manifesto was changed. Thesis 6 was made to read: "We assert that the time has passed for theism, deism, modernism and the several varieties of 'new thought.' If traditional religious words such as god, salvation and soul are retained at all they must be unambiguously defined and used, without reservation, to symbolize verifiable scientific knowledge and empirically discoverable human values."

Now Robert Morss Lovett in checking the draft is rather scathing in denouncing that statement. I send you a copy of what he has to say. It is really quite funny and I am aware that you know Lovett. In other particulars we followed your suggestions almost to the word. Won't you comment on this number Six and Lovett's reaction to it? Could not we let it stand very simply as a flat assertion without ruling out those other possibilities?

Perhaps it will be best for me to include a copy of the Manifesto as we drew it up, the copy prior to Lovett's check for form, etc. You will realize that there have been some changes in punctuation and a scattered word here and there. Send me your comment soon. We are eager to get it out in the near future.

Dr. Burtt replied on April 26:

Lovett's comment on the sixth thesis is certainly an illuminating illustration of the impossibility of telling in advance what words are going to mean to anybody. What I had essentially in mind in the modifications I suggested in the fifth and sixth theses was that there are many liberal religionists who still feel that they can give genuine meaning to traditional terms that have been associated with theistic or at least modernistic points of view, but who are yet entirely at one with humanism in what I take to be its decisive emphases, such as unreserved commitment to scientific method, determination of value by intelligent assessment of human experiences of good, and an uncompromising stand on the social and economic problem. It seemed to me important that any such should be welcomed and not repelled by the manifesto. I do not agree entirely with such people, but at the same time I am not committed to an extreme naturalism, and think it would be a great pity for the manifesto to imply more radical doctrines in this direction than is necessary for an unreserved stand on the things that humanism does count vital. That you and your friends agree with this as a general policy I assume from your kindly response to my previous letter.

How would it do to restate the sixth thesis as follows: "We believe that the time has passed for theism, deism, modernism, and the several varieties of new thought. At the same time we welcome religious fellowship with any who interpret the human quest for the highest values in terms which have been associated with these positions (such as God, salvation, soul, and the like), as long as the interpretation is consistent with insistence on scientific method as the only sound guide to truth and on intelligent, democratic criticism of human experiences of good as the only dependable guide to ideals of value." This is somewhat awkward and needs smoothing in detail, but you will see my guiding idea. By the way, the fifteenth thesis also seems to me awkward, especially the second sentence. Can't someone improve and clarify it a bit? I have no concrete suggestion, but I don't quite like it. Another minor point— the first sentence of the last paragraph of the manifesto might seem to some readers a bit melodramatic. Would not this be better: "As religious humanists we stand on the above theses."

I appreciate deeply your genial response to my suggestions and shall be eager to see the public reaction to the manifesto when it appears.

On the basis of this important comment by Dr. Burtt, some final changes were made. Dr. Burtt's interest in Western scientific and religious humanism diminished some years later, following his studies in the Orient and his considerable interest in Buddhism. However, his contribution to the evolution of "A Humanist Manifesto" was substantial, and his views of the movement five years later appear in the first edition of his *Types of Religious Philosophy*, in which he devotes about forty-five pages to religious humanism as a further development of modernism.

CHAPTER 10

The Search for Signers — Round Two

With the editorial process completed, "A Humanist Manifesto" was ready to submit to a wider group of signers as a finished document. The considerations that went into deciding who to invite and who not to invite to endorse it were many. After much discussion, a list of prospective signatories was drawn up by at least three of the editorial committee (Bragg, Reese, and myself) and serves as a key to our outlook in 1933 on the scope of the emerging humanist movement in the United States, as seen from Chicago.

The initial handwritten list was drafted at a meeting, then supplemented with other names including James Harvey Robinson, C. Hartley Grattan, Walter Lippman, Clarence Darrow, T. V. Smith, Irwin Edman, Charles Beard, and Lewis Mumford, among others. With the exception of some very minor changes in punctuation, the final draft went out to approximately sixty-five persons in essentially the same form in which it was ultimately published. Thirty-four of those persons signed in time for publication (the Reverend Alson Robinson's signature came in late).

A 54 percent return was not bad for a movement that had not yet crystallized into a formal organization. It wasn't until 1935 that the Humanist Press Association, Inc., was formed to finance *The New Humanist*, the humanist movement's primary vehicle for outreach. Humanism was a movement just beginning to surface as an explicit position in

American religious thought, and the thirty-four who signed the manifesto—and indeed the viewpoint of the manifesto itself—did not fully measure the dimensions of humanism in 1933. In time, adjectives other than *religious* would be applied to humanism, and many other emphases would be brought forward.

The reader should remember the haste involved in the selective process necessitated by the pressure of the press release and publication deadline. Clearly, the limitations of the editors' personal attitudes, contacts, reading, and experience were a factor in selecting the list of potential signers.

One Woman

Examination of the list of invited signers raises many questions. One is the absence of women's names, which, from today's perspective, seems shocking. But it reflects the limitations of awareness in the 1930s. The humanist movement—like culture in general—reflected a male chauvinist climate from which, more than six decades later, American society has not fully emerged.

There was one exception to the male-dominated list of potential signers: Mary MacDowell, a contemporary of Jane Addams involved in Chicago social work. That her name was included, and in the handwriting of Dr. Curtis Reese, is entirely understandable; Reese was dean of the Abraham Lincoln Center in Chicago, a social welfare agency with informal ties to the Western Unitarian Conference, where he had become influential in his leadership of social workers. Mary MacDowell's inclusion as the sole female on the list may indicate that in 1933 humanists were perhaps vaguely aware of feminism and its affinity to humanism. It does indicate the high regard we felt for her. Recently, we came into possession of a picture of thirteen Unitarian ministers, including Lester Mondale, Raymond Bragg, Curtis Reese, and myself, with Mary MacDowell as an honored guest.

The Unitarians

Why some persons were not on the list of invited signers is as significant as why some were. I've already covered several people who sent us their comments on the early draft, declining to sign. And although we had no direct personal contact with some who were omitted, no doubt we were guided by their published writings.

Over half of those who signed "A Humanist Manifesto" were Unitarians. However, there were Unitarians who did not sign, including Robert J. Hutcheon, a professor at the Meadville Theological School. Both Bragg and I had studied under him, and he was obviously asked as a courtesy. (Hutcheon is not to be confused with Robert Maynard Hutchins, then president of the University of Chicago.) Professor Hutcheon's views are expressed in his 1929 book, *Frankness in Religion*, in which he affirmed a "conviction concerning the eternal worth and the cosmic support of values." It was his aim "to save for humanity the essential spiritual values which religious faith, and especially the Christian form which it creates." He declared: "We must lay hold on something outside ourselves to lift ourselves to the height of our spiritual being. . . ." This was in contrast to the temper and conviction of the religious humanists of the time that there was no cosmic guarantee of their values and that it was, to coin a phrase from Erich Fromm, "man for himself." Throughout his teaching career at Meadville, Dr. Hutcheon struggled vigorously with classes of students in a school that regularly graduated a good percentage of humanists.

If Dr. Hutcheon was asked to sign the manifesto as a matter of courtesy, you may wonder why Professor Charles H. Lyttle, another member of the Meadville faculty, was not also invited. After all, he contributed to the development of humanism through his book *Freedom Moves West*, which includes a sympathetic review of the rise of humanism in the context of liberal religion. As well, he encouraged a number of students to write their theses on phases of the humanist position and development. As his former students, Bragg and I were aware of his unwavering wish not to label himself and of his opposition to anything that might become a creed, and I suspect we did not invite Lyttle to sign as a gesture of courtesy.

Another Unitarian minister whose name was included on the list, although at the time he had left the active ministry, was Everett Dean Martin. He and Curtis Reese had both had churches in Iowa. Dr. Reese felt that Martin had pioneered for democratic religion in essentially humanist concepts, although without the label. Martin, however, was unresponsive and, from about that time, was not heard of again in Unitarian circles. Within any denomination, mystery often surrounds the departure of a minister from the profession.

Another person appearing in Unitarian pulpits as a lecturer and using the unpatentable label *humanist* was Edward Howard Griggs. His book *The New Humanism: Studies in Personal and Social Development* was first copyrighted in 1899 and, by 1922, had reached its eighth edition. Griggs was on the list to receive an invitation to sign, but there is real doubt as to whether he was ever located. He belonged to the background from which the 1933 "Humanist Manifesto" emerged, but the influence of science was not obvious in his writings. His work seems more like a foreshadowing of the backward- and inward-looking "new humanism" (or literary humanism) of Irving Babbitt and Paul Elmer More, but with an added perspective derived from the always culturally rich and socially concious Unitarianism of eastern United States.

The Reverend Alfred Cole was on the list of invitees; however, he declined to sign. The Unitarian minister was later identified with the humanist movement through his creative work in collating and publishing service material consonant with the humanist outlook. He later signed *Humanist Manifesto II*.

It's a mystery why some other Unitarians were not asked to sign "A Humanist Manifesto." Despite devoting his life to the gathering and writing of humanistically oriented liberal service material, especially hymns, the Reverend Vincent Silliman was not asked. Neither was the Reverend Frank Waring, who was an outspoken humanist. Raymond Bragg wrote to me in 1973 that he remembered Waring vividly, that Waring had visited his Chicago office, but that he could not recall which churches Waring had served.

Others equally outspoken by 1933 whose names were not on our list of invitees include the Reverend Rupert Holloway, later minister at Madison, Wisconsin, who authored several early articles in *The New Humanist*. In fact, one of his articles, "The Mystical Mood," appeared in the same issue in which "A Humanist Manifesto" was published.

And George G. Davis, an official of the American Unitarian Association, was not on the original list but was subsequently asked to sign the manifesto. He declined.

The Reverend Walton E. Cole of Toledo, Ohio—at that time considered a humanist—was also sent the confidential draft. He had been minister of the Third Unitarian Church of Chicago; I succeeded him when he left to go to Toledo. I cite Cole as typical of the success-minded career preachers, including a number of humanist ministers who reverted to theism, sometimes departing from Unitarian pulpits for Congregational or Methodist settlements. "You'll see, Ed, who gets the big churches," one careerist told me. I felt that in certain cases these apostates were rationalizing a new technique for success.

Among these former humanists there were undoubtedly others who cherished the richness of the Christian tradition, including its music, art, and liturgy. Walton Cole liked expensive oil paintings and imported sports cars. He went from a Unitarian ministry in Toledo to the Second Church of Boston, with its modified Episcopal service, a processional of eight robed choir members, as well as a flag bearer and a cross bearer. The records show no response from Cole to the invitation to sign, but as he described his career change later, he "went where the people were" and tried to fulfill the needs of a large Congregational Church in Detroit, including the symbolism that clergy and ritual so often provide. In later correspondence, Cole wrote that he had finally come back into Unitarianism and was at the humanist position again.

The Reverend Hugh S. Tigner of Oneonta, New York, was another Unitarian with reportedly humanist views whom

Bragg had contacted early on. In an April 5, 1933, letter Tigner wrote Bragg:

> I wish to thank you for the Humanist Manifesto and for the opportunity of signing it. But I am not taking advantage of that opportunity for several reasons, a few of which I will take the trouble to briefly indicate. In the first place, the manifesto—particularly the first five or six affirmations—is repugnant to me, not because I directly disagree with it, but because it does not contain the proper sense of humility. For example, it is asserted that "the nature of the universe depicted by modern science. . . ." That's utterly ridiculous. Granted that the findings of science are of the greatest significance, these findings only scratch the surface of the universe, and certainly they do not tell us what the *nature* of the universe is. I know of no scientist who makes such a preposterous claim. The nature of the universe is just as much a mystery today as it was 20,000 years ago, and it looks as though man will never devise an instrument for prying into the mystery.
>
> In the second place, I am tired of signing manifestoes [*sic*] of this sort. I am in full agreement with the aims of Humanism; but what is Humanism's program for achieving these aims? That is what I am interested in. So long as Humanism remains in the arm-chair stage seeing visions in its pipe-smoke (and I see no indications of it doing anything else) it does not inspire me enough to say that I am interested in it. I fail to see how Humanism is more worthwhile than liberal Christianity—the last word in ineffectuality.
>
> In the third place, Humanism is an academic religion. It emerges from no vital social experience, no vital social movement. It is, therefore, not the answer to modern man's spiritual needs. It may please a few anemic professors, and it is well suited to the more thoughtful and honest adherents of liberal religion, but it has not yet succeeded in finding the new pattern of spiritual life which the present world is instinctively crying out for. I regard Humanism as Mr. Hoover did Prohibition, as "a noble experiment."
>
> These remarks are critical, but I assure you that they are made in a friendly spirit. Several years ago I called myself a Humanist. I think I understand Humanism. I do

not flatly disagree with any of Humanism's assertions or denials, but I cannot see that Humanism leads anywhere. It does not contain what I am looking for. I admit that I am still looking. I find Humanists more congenial to my viewpoint than liberal Christians, but I confess that both bore me.

One wonders what the other earlier manifestos were that had made Tigner tired of signing.

The Philosophers

Philosophers—particularly Roy Wood Sellars, Edwin A. Burtt, Max C. Otto, John Dewey, and John H. Randall, Jr.— were prominent among the signers of "A Humanist Manifesto" in 1933. One distinguished name that was on the list of invitees but missing from the signers was Dr. Corliss Lamont. When asked in 1972 why he had not signed the manifesto, Lamont replied, "I have no idea. I wish I had." There clearly must have been a breakdown in communication.

Dr. Lamont's books have been widely read within the humanist movement. Among the most prominent are *The Philosophy of Humanism* (for which I wrote the foreword in the 1965 fifth edition), *The Illusion of Immortality* (for which John Dewey wrote the preface), and *Freedom Is As Freedom Does*, a volume expressing Lamont's views as a consistent proponent of civil liberties. (Lamont also consulted with me in Chicago concerning the publication in 1936 of his excellent volume, *Man Answers Death: An Anthology of Poetry*, which included a few poems added at my suggestion.)

Another philosopher who had his feet firmly planted on the earth and was completely oriented toward democratic values and method was Thomas Vernor Smith. Although Smith most certainly contributed to the stream of thought that surfaced in "A Humanist Manifesto," he never formally labeled himself a humanist. In his 1926 book *The Democratic Way of Life*, he presented a vague concept of a humanmade deity not unlike the concept of his distinguished colleague at the University of Chicago, Edward Scribner Ames. This deity was, according to Smith, a projection of the ideals, values, and experience of the group. Smith wrote: "Where two or three are gathered together in friendship, their deity arises among them; if they add to their number, deity is expanded, and if they can include all men in the charmed circle of their friendliness, they have created a world-God as citizens of the world." One can only assume that Smith was not asked to sign because of the 1933 manifesto's compilers' sharp break with "God language." I believe that Smith's books were humanistic in the broader sense and certainly they were influential. Among those which I reviewed were *Beyond Conscience* and *Creative Skeptics*, both published in 1934.

Smith and I kept in touch intermittently. I am still impressed with the prediction he made when he came through Salt Lake City sometime shortly after 1946. He said to me: "The church-state issue will make the front pages of the American press again and again for a hundred years." Apparently, he knew the lesson of history concerning the Roman church: "*Le plus ce change, le plus c'est le meme*" (the more things change, the more they stay the same). Later in his career, Smith was elected to the U.S. Congress as a representative.

Dr. Harry Overstreet was asked to sign the manifesto, but his wife, Bonaro, was not. I suspect this oversight is a result of the male insensitivity of the day. Eventually they both belonged to the American Humanist Association. After 1941, when the publication of *The New Humanist* was resumed as *The Humanist* and I was editor, Dr. Overstreet and Dr. Edwin A. Burtt called on me in Schenectady to encourage my work.

There are no records in the files to indicate evidence that Dr. Overstreet ever responded to the invitation to sign the first manifesto. Later he dropped out of the AHA as he had become preoccupied with the threat of Stalinism. He seemed to feel that any publication that did not align itself in the Cold War was suspect.

Irwin Edman, whose 1938 *Philosopher's Holiday* has delighted many people, was considered by Curtis Reese to be a humanist. To our knowledge he never made a humanist commitment organizationally but was part of the humanistic influence stemming from Columbia University.

One of the most caustic letters we received came from British Professor F. C. S. Schiller. In 1927, I audited Schiller's lectures at Oxford University. Reese, who left many of his books to me, had obviously read, marked, and inwardly digested Schiller's writings on humanism, including *Studies in Humanism* and *Humanism: Philosophical Essays.* Schiller's books contain valuable material on the beginnings and background of humanism, especially concerning Protagorous. I can still hear Schiller's sonorous pronouncements on "The Confounding of the Absolute."

Biting sarcasm came through Schiller's letter, written from California on University Club of Los Angeles stationery in response to our invitation to sign the manifesto. I've often wondered whether Schiller was adopting the attitude *"L'humanisme c'est moi."* Might he have been defending his assumption that he was at the top of the pecking order in humanist history and that new voices on the topic were invading his field? The views of George Sarton, Will Durant, J. A. C. F. Auer, and others on this would have been valuable but, alas, they died too soon like many pioneers in the field, including Schiller. I was deeply disappointed at the tone of Schiller's refusal to sign, particularly because he was someone I had admired and respected. Schiller wrote on April 16:

> You sent me your invitation to sign your Humanist Manifesto on Apr. 6 with an invitation "that signatures had to be received by not later than Apr. 10th", so presumably you merely wished to inform me of its contents or perhaps expected me to express an opinion about it. Now I have expressed my opinion about your sort of "Humanism" in the article I have contributed to the Encyclopedia of the Social Sciences, Vol. VII, and there is, I think, nothing in your Manifesto which requires me to modify it. I note that your manifesto has 15 articles, 50% more than the Ten Commandments and one more even than President Wilson's Fourteen Points. Its general attitude is that of what was formerly, and adequately, described as Positivism, and

seems to be a form of Naturalism. So the propriety of the name Humanism is not apparent to me. Regarded as a religious program it seems to me to suffer from vagueness and weakness on its constructive side, and it seems difficult to understand why any one holding its views should wish to associate himself in an organization with others holding similar opinions. But undoubtedly man is a very social and sociable animal! Believe me.

The Social Scientists

From the perspective of more than fifty years later, we wonder now that there were not more social scientists invited to sign the manifesto. One reason may be that, in their effort to be scientific, some social scientists in the 1920s and early 1930s were trying to mimic the objectivity of the physical scientists and became dehumanized in the process. Some sociologists were expressing disinterest in or irresponsibility toward the uses to which the knowledge produced by their research and experiments was to be applied. After taking six graduate sociology courses at the University of Chicago, with an eye to a career in sociology, I turned my thoughts back to the liberal churches and ministry because there I found concern for human well-being and development that I had not found among sociologists.

There was one social scientist, William Amberson, who was asked to sign "A Humanist Manifesto." He had been editor of the *Journal of Social Psychology*; however, just like the journal, he just seemed to have dropped out of sight.

James Harvey Robinson's stance, as expressed in his *The Mind in the Making*, was one of openness to new ideas and change. "Nothing is going to be settled in the way in which things were supposed to be settled, for the simple reason that knowledge will probably continue to increase and will inevitably alter the world in which we have come to terms." Written in 1921, these words characterize the temper of the years preceding "A Humanist Manifesto." In his little book *The Humanizing of Knowledge*, Robinson held it necessary to resynthesize knowledge and pointed to its uses in the interests of human welfare. He was a leading protagonist of precise thought and exact knowledge and its widespread dissemination in contrast to "modes of thinking repugnant to scientific intelligence" as found in traditional supernaturalism. Not forgetting the publishing influence of the British-based Rationalist Press Association, no single book inspired me more as editor and disseminator of humanist publications and literature for nearly half a century than this small volume. But James Harvey Robinson did not sign "A Humanist Manifesto," nor did he respond to the letter of invitation.

The Spectrum Widened

Among the others asked to sign but who did not were an economist, a judge, an attorney, two historians, a literary critic, a journalist, and Paul Blanshard—who fits several of these categories. The variety of individuals who were invited to sign clearly demonstrates that we editors were at least attempting to achieve a certain breadth to the spectrum of signatories.

Frank H. Knight, an economist at the University of Chicago, declined to sign, entering a vociferous objection to the inclusion or the endorsement of language that stated a need for "a radical change in methods, controls, and motives" of "an acquisitive and profit-motivated society." Point fourteen was then and is now controversial. Its inclusion in 1933 is easy to understand given the ongoing economic depression of that decade, particularly since the New Deal had not yet been proposed.

Judge Ben Lindsay was on the list to be asked, but no response from him is in the record. In about 1925, Judge Lindsay had lectured on his proposed "companionate marriage" in a Methodist church in Meadville, Pennsylvania, with the entire student body from Meadville Theological School in attendance. The judge—fifty years ahead of his time—was something of a hero to that group.

Literary critic C. Hartley Grattan was asked to sign the

manifesto because of his editing of a broadside against the literary humanism. *The Critique of Humanism*, published in 1930, examined the work, *Humanism and America*, edited by Norman Foerster and also published in 1930 and containing essays by Irving Babbitt, Paul Elmore More, an T. S. Eliot. Among those aligned with Grattan in his counterattack were Allen Tate, Kenneth Burke, Lewis Mumford, Malcolm Cowley, and Edmund Wilson.

Grattan did not respond to our invitation to sign the manifesto. My theory is that the title of *The New Humanist* publication sponsoring "A Humanist Manifesto" repelled these critics of reactionary literary humanism, which also clamed to be the "new humanism." It took a decade and a simplified title for the journal (dropping the word *new*) for naturalistic humanists—both scientific and religious—to clear away the confusion over the word *humanism* caused by the literary struggle of the time.

Another who did not reply was Walter Lippmann. His 1929 book *A Preface to Morals*, which dealt with the "acids of modernity" that were eroding belief in the Judeo-Christian theology, was widely read by humanists.

Why Paul Blanshard did not sign the manifesto is also a mystery. I can only speculate that his political activities as a comptroller of the City of New York prevented him from responding. His collaboration with me at *The Humanist* dates from the late 1940s when *The Nation* was excluded from New York City's high school libraries by the board of education because of Blanshard's series on Roman Catholic clericalism and its demand for public subsidy of parochial schools. Paul Blanshard took over my column in *The Humanist* entitled "The Sectarian Battlefront" and continued to write for the magazine almost until his death in January 1980. He also lectured extensively on behalf of both the magazine and the American Humanist Association.

Clarence Darrow was an obvious person to ask for his signature. In his *The Story of My Life*, he wrote of his parents move to Meadville, Pennsylvania:

On one hill in Meadville stood Allegheny College, sponsored by the Methodist Church. On another elevation was a Unitarian seminary, and in the town was a Unitarian Church. Both my parents must have stayed to this church, for when my father's time had come to take a theological course he went to the Unitarian school in Meaville, on the other hill from the Methodist College, where he took his first degree. In due time he completed his theological course, but when he had finished his studies he found that he had lost his faith. Even the mild tenets of Unitarianism he could not accept. Unitarianism, then, was closer to Orthodoxy than it is today, or he might have been a clergyman and lived an easier life. In the Unitarian school he read Newman and Channing, but later went on to Emerson and Theodore Parker. His trend of mind was shown by the fact that his first son was Edward Everett. When it came my turn to be born and named, my parents had left the Unitarian faith behind and were sailing out on the open sea without a rudder or compass, and with no port in sight, and so I could not be named after any prominent Unitarian.

At the time of Darrow's death, rumor of his alleged (but false) deathbed conversion to Christianity was promptly circulated by Christian zealots. When I called on his widow as a Unitarian minister, Mrs. Darrow told me, in effect, that her husband would not enter a church. However, there are reports of Darrow having lectured at a Universalist church. He did not respond to the invitation to sign the manifesto. Eventually, his law partner, William H. Holly (when a judge), joined the American Humanist Association.

I have tried to demonstrate in this sampling of people asked and not asked to sign that the scope and influence of humanism was far wider than indicated by the manifesto signers. However, the fact that thirty-four widely dispersed and unorganized humanists agreed upon the document would seem to make it a real achievement in consensus by a small volunteer committee with no budget.

CHAPTER 11

Distinctions Between Literary and Religious Humanism

In retrospect, I think it was inevitable that some persons would be overlooked who should have been asked to sign the manifesto and others asked whose positions were not fully known. We were, after all, working under pressure, with no budget, and with very little clerical help.

Two important educators who contributed to the discussion of humanism before 1933 but who were not asked to sign the manifesto were Edward Scribner Ames and Oscar W. Firkins. Dr. Ames taught philosophy at the University of Chicago, and Dr. Firkins taught English at the University of Minnesota. These two men helped distinguish the new *religious humanism*—which was naturalistic in philosophy, socially activist in sympathies, and scientific in orientation—from a so-called *literary humanism*, which was at that time widely known and specifically identified with the viewpoints of Irving Babbitt and Paul Elmer More. Along with many others, I felt that the literary humanists had misappropriated the term *humanism*, as their position was elitist and they were committed neither to humanitarian reforms nor social change. Whereas religious humanists saw science as an important tool in fulfilling the potential for a better life, the literary humanists were anti-science; in fact, they outwardly rejected science. In the March/April 1931 issue of *The New Humanist*, Firkins described literary humanism as having a "background [that] is scholarly, its basis is introspective and retrospective; it looks into its own soul; and it combats that side of the present which strikes it as inimical to the testimony of the ages and of its own soul."

Interestingly, literary humanism turned out to be a short-lived fad that didn't survive the decade. It bears mentioning now only because, in the 1930s, religious humanism was frequently mistaken for or misunderstood as a part of the literary humanism movement. It turns out that, in describing our naturalistic humanism as "new" and having the movement's (albeit) unofficial magazine name *The "New" Humanist*, we unwittingly contributed to the confusion.

Edward Scribner Ames

Because of my feeling that Edward Scribner Ames was one of the very great men on the University of Chicago campus, I took his course "The Psychology of Religious Experience" during the summer of 1929 while completing work for a master's degree in comparative religions under A. Eustace Haydon. I revered Dr. Ames while he was my teacher and found him to be a thorough-going naturalist despite his use of traditional theistic terms. (I once heard Professor Ames say sadly to a young Disciples of Christ minister, who had lost his pulpit for refraining from the use of traditional terms, "If you had listened to me, you could still be there.")

However, there is no question of the sincerity or validity of Dr. Ames' beliefs; his views were based on profound psychological study of religious experience. Anyone who ever heard Edward Scribner Ames lecture would be immensely impressed. I can still remember, at the end of the course, saying to him: "If I have a god, I want a *real* god!" Feigning intimidation by shaking his fist in my face, Professor Ames thundered in reply: "My God *is* a *real* god!"

In 1931, Ames set forth his views in a lecture to the Chicago Literary Club, which was also published as a brochure entitled *Humanism:*

[Religious] humanists are naturalistic, experimental, be-

havioristic, humanitarian. They accept the evolutionary
doctrine. . . . This sphere (here and now) of human interests and accomplishments is the proper concern of many,
according to these humanists. . . . (a) chief point of attack of the humanist upon the old beliefs is the existence
of God, and in general the conception of the supernatural
which runs through those beliefs. . . . They emphasize the
function of scientific knowledge as a means of realizing
a better and happier life.

The editors of "A Humanist Manifesto" were all familiar with
this Chicago Literary Club discussion of what Ames termed
"a new *ism*." Reviewing its historical background and discussing the so-called humanism of Irving Babbitt and his disciples—especially Paul Elmer More, who "does not hesitate
to go the whole distance in the acceptance of supernatural
religion and traditional theology"—Ames usefully presented
the literary humanists of the 1930s as "violently opposed not
only to Rousseau but to Francis Bacon and John Dewey."
Ames stated of Babbitt and More:

Bacon, for them, symbolizes empirical science and the
spirit of our machine age, in which his motto, "Knowledge is power," leads to the . . . naturalism and pragmatism of John Dewey. It is not strange, then, to hear these
[new] humanists proclaim that they [Babbitt and More] are
reactionaries in the midst of the modernists.

Many humanists, myself included, have long felt that
naturalistic (scientific) humanism can be traced back directly
to Bacon's *Novum Organum*, first published in 1620, and his
argument that we should "pursue science in order that human
life may be enhanced."

Dr. Ames gave his own notion of the gods as something
real but which has grown out of human group experience:
"The gods are not separate from men but are of one nature
with them. Gods and men constitute one living organism,
one kinship group." To Ames, God was apparently a projection of this group spirit: "Projections of new ideas of God
have appeared in the midst of social readjustment. . . . God

and man are moving together out of the old dualistic framework of an outworn religious philosophy into a living social process where their kinship and common nature are better understood."

In spite of his brochure's title, *Humanism*, Ames in effect read himself out of the new movement because of his concept of God. Understandably, the manifesto editors did not ask Edward Scribner Ames to sign because it was their view that any use of supernatural symbols or god language would open the door to a flood of theist apologists. An explicit nontheism refraining from the use of traditional theological language was the distinguishing feature of the newer humanists. Later, when the word-conscious pioneers were more ecumenical and not as severe in their use of language, I think it certain that a man of Ames' caliber would have been included. Using the term *ecumenical* as being unity in the cause of humankind, as compared to unity in God and Christ, the humanists of 1973 who worked on and signed the second manifesto did not maintain as sharp a symbolic barrier as did the editors of "A Humanist Manifesto" in 1933.

Though not asked to sign the manifesto, Dr. Ames was respected. And I'll always remember a comment he made to me during a visit to his home (this was much later, after he had retired and after having had both legs amputated): "Here I sit, literally footless, wondering what it would be like if—as I do not believe—it were possible for me to rejoin the wife of my years in an existence other than this."

Oscar W. Firkins

Oscar W. Firkins, an English professor at the University of Minnesota, published a comparison of the humanism of John Dietrich and that of the literary humanists entitled "The Two Humanisms: A Discrimination" (*The New Humanist*, March/April 1931). These "two cults," as he called them, "co-exist quite without coherence; almost without collision." Of that time's better-known Babbitt-More humanism, he wrote: "The Tennysonian 'self-reverence, self-knowledge, self-control' conveys much of its spirit. Briefly and loosely, it stands for inward discipline grounded on a sifted tradition; its inwardness tends to distrust science; its discipline is hostile to romance."

I suspect that it was an oversight that Dr. Firkins was not asked to sign "A Humanist Manifesto." His response would have been interesting. Of the two humanisms—literary and religious—Firkins concluded: "Each has an intuition as a basis. The faith in reason as savior is, after all, a faith; the future, its chosen witness, holds its tongue."

CHAPTER 12

Responses to the Final Draft

Having taken into consideration both the criticisms and suggestions we received, the final draft was completed and sent to everyone who had agreed to sign, as well as to the principal advance critics. The responses to the draft were diverse. Some authorizations to sign came by wire in order to meet the deadline. The files show that the earlier versions had been approved by most signers.

Albert Dieffenbach wrote, "The draft is now excellent."

Professor Robert Morss Lovett wrote, "I am proud to be able to sign the Humanist Manifesto, so sound in thought and admirable in expression."

Charles Francis Potter wrote to me on April 28 from New York City and volunteered to handle press releases there.

Llewellyn Jones, a Chicago literary critic who was later to become editor of the Unitarian publication then called the *Christian Register*, wrote: "I am glad to see that the Manifesto was against profit motivation. That plank seems to indicate that we mean what we say in other planks."

Unofficially representing Universalism, Clinton Lee Scott wrote: " I am glad to sign the Humanist Manifesto. It probably represents as well as any one statement could a cross section of the thought of the number of persons included, but I make the familiar reservation, 'Neither this nor any other precise form of words etc.' " (Scott refers here to the escape clause customarily used by religious liberals in any effort to present a consensus of their faith.) He continued: "One of the primary virtues of a Humanist is his intellectual modesty. Whether the universe is 'self-existing' or 'created,' and whether or not there is a cosmic end beyond the fulfillment of man's life here and now are matters about which even a Theist can make but a poor guess. However, I like the positive character of the statement and especially the recognition of the economic factors."

Clearly some who signed "A Humanist Manifesto" did so reluctantly, disagreeing on particular points.

David Rhys Williams took exception to point three, which deals with body-soul dualism. On April 14, Bragg wrote to Williams: "There seems to be a good deal of sentiment similar to your own in regard to the Third Thesis." Williams' explicit objections do not appear in the files, but a wire came from him the same day as Bragg's letter was mailed authorizing the use of his signature. Williams later renounced the humanist position, attacking its nontheism.

Lester Mondale signed the manifesto but included a statement questioning the all-out naturalistic metaphysic of the document. A Unitarian minister, Mondale succeeded Raymond Bragg in the Evanston, Illinois, pulpit and was the youngest of all the signers.[1]

Not everyone signed the final draft. On April 24, 1933, the manifesto editors received another very significant letter—this from Rabbi Joseph L. Baron of the Congregation Emanu-El B'ne Jeshuran in Milwaukee, Wisconsin. Bragg had sent the draft to Baron at the suggestion of Eustace Haydon. Baron responded:

> I appreciate the compliment implied in your communication of April 15th, and I regret that I cannot join with you in signing the Humanist Manifesto. Speaking only with reference to the Jewish group, I consider the issuance of such a statement at the present time as ill-advised.
>
> I might take exception to some of your conclusions. For instance, I find the concept of the self-existence of the

---

1. As of November 1995, Lester Mondale is the only surviving manifesto signer.

universe just as unintelligible as that of its creation. I find your statement with regard to mind as a function of the organism as too simple and terse to do justice to the viewpoint of vitalism. But my criticism is based on the spirit and purport of the manifesto as a whole rather than on any of its details.

I believe that it is a repressive and futile effort to establish a uniformity of opinion in a dynamic religious movement, particularly at such an early stage in its development. The best we may do in this direction is to point out certain tendencies, and not to clinch it with a new dogmatism.

Your manifesto ignores some personal effects of the old forms of piety which are a vital need in the life of many members of the Jewish group, to say nothing of the Christian, whose arrogant, vulgar and selfish reaction to the conditions of our environment makes it necessary that we follow a conservative and not a radical process in changing the meaning of holiness.

Your stress on metaphysical affirmations and denials may inject a theological polemic in liberal synagogues, where the membership is not concerned with the definition of God or of the hereafter but with practical problems such as the application of the ideals of justice and peace, the upbuilding of a Jewish civilization in Palestine, the combat against tyranny and fanaticism, etc. To divert the attention of the Jewish congregation, and to divide its forces, by declarations against "theism, deism, modernism, and new thought," would be an unfortunate obstacle in the path of its humanistic leaders who are endeavoring to mobilize its strength toward the achievement of "a socialized and cooperative" way of life.

By no means should a signature on the manifesto be equated with 100 percent agreement but, rather, it signifies an approximate consensus. Even though some signers did not specify as much, we can take for granted that they had some reservations or took exception to various fine points in the language. But we must assume that the signers of the manifesto found themselves in substantial agreement with the tone, the direction, and the basic assumptions of the document.

CHAPTER 13

Publication of
"A Humanist Manifesto"

In desperation to meet the deadline for *The New Humanist* in which "A Humanist Manifesto" would first appear publicly, I crossed the last "t" and dotted the final "i," making some purely minor typographical corrections, and sent it to the printer. I did this even though Bragg and I had begun to question the wisdom of using the word *manifesto*.

The text of "A Humanist Manifesto" is reprinted here precisely as it appeared in the May/June 1933 issue of *The New Humanist* (VI:3:1–5). The thirty-four endorsers signed as individuals and their organizational or professional connections were given for identification only.

A Humanist Manifesto

The time has come for widespread recognition of the radical changes in religious beliefs throughout the modern world. The time is past for mere revision of traditional attitudes. Science and economic change have disrupted the old beliefs. Religions the world over are under the necessity of coming to terms with new conditions created by a vastly increased knowledge and experience. In every field of human activity, the vital movement is now in the direction of a candid and explicit humanism. In order that religious humanism may be better understood we, the undersigned, desire to make certain affirmations which we believe the facts of our contemporary life demonstrate.

There is great danger of a final, and we believe fatal, identification of the word *religion* with doctrines and methods which have lost their significance and which are powerless to solve the problems of human living in the Twentieth Century. Religions have always been means for realizing the highest values of life. Their end has been accomplished through the interpretation of the total environing situation (theology or world view), the sense of values resulting therefrom (goal or ideal), and the technique (cult), established for realizing the satisfactory life. A change in any of these factors results in alteration of the outward forms of religion. This fact explains the changefulness of religions throughout the centuries. But through all changes religion itself remains constant in its quest for abiding values, an inseparable feature of human life.

Today man's larger understanding of the universe, his scientific achievements, and his deeper appreciation of brotherhood have created a situation which requires a new statement of the means and purposes of religion. Such a vital, fearless, and frank religion capable of furnishing adequate social goals and personal satisfactions may appear to many people as a complete break with the past. While this age does owe a vast debt to the traditional religions, it is nonetheless obvious that any religion that can hope to be a synthesizing and dynamic force for today must be shaped for the needs of this age. To establish such a religion is a major necessity of the present. It is a responsibility which rests upon this generation. We therefore affirm the following:

First: Religious humanists regard the universe as self-existing and not created.

Second: Humanism believes that man is a part of nature and that he has emerged as the result of a continuous process.

Third: Holding an organic view of life, humanists find that the traditional dualism of mind and body must be rejected.

Fourth: Humanism recognizes that man's religious culture and civilization, as clearly depicted by anthropology and history, are the product of a gradual development due to his interaction with his natural environment and with his social heritage. The individual born into a particular culture is largely molded by that culture.

Fifth: Humanism asserts that the nature of the universe depicted by modern science makes unacceptable any supernatural or cosmic guarantees of human values. Obviously humanism does not deny the possibility of realities as yet undiscovered, but it does insist that the way to determine the existence and value of any and all realities is by means of intelligent inquiry and by the assessment of their relation to human needs. Religion must formulate its hopes and plans in the light of the scientific spirit and method.

Sixth: We are convinced that the time has passed for theism, deism, modernism, and the several varieties of "new thought."

Seventh: Religion consists of those actions, purposes, and experiences which are humanly significant. Nothing human is alien to the religious. It includes labor, art, science, philosophy, love, friendship, recreation—all that is in its degree expressive of intelligently satisfying human living. The distinction between the sacred and the secular can no longer be maintained.

Eighth: Religious humanism considers the complete realization of human personality to be the end of man's life and seeks its development and fulfillment in the here and now. This is the explanation of the humanist's social passion.

Ninth: In place of the old attitudes involved in worship and prayer the humanist finds his religious emotions expressed in a heightened sense of personal life and in a cooperative effort to promote social well-being.

Tenth: It follows that there will be no uniquely religious emotions and attitudes of the kind hitherto associated with belief in the supernatural.

Eleventh: Man will learn to face the crises of life in terms of his knowledge of their naturalness and probability. Reasonable and manly attitudes will be fostered by education and supported by custom. We assume that humanism will take the path of social and mental hygiene and discourage sentimental and unreal hopes and wishful thinking.

Twelfth: Believing that religion must work increasingly for joy in living, religious humanists aim to foster the creative in man and to encourage achievements that add to the satisfactions of life.

Thirteenth: Religious humanism maintains that all associations and institutions exist for the fulfillment of human life. The intelligent evaluation, transformation, control, and direction of such associations and institutions with a view to the enhancement of human life is the purpose and program of humanism. Certainly religious institutions, their ritualistic forms, ecclesiastical methods, and communal activities must be reconstituted as rapidly as experience allows, in order to function effectively in the modern world.

Fourteenth: The humanists are firmly convinced that existing acquisitive and profit-motivated society has shown itself to be inadequate and that a radical change in methods, controls, and motives must be instituted. A socialized and cooperative economic order must be established to the end that the equitable distribution of the means of life be possible. The goal of humanism is a free and universal society in which people voluntarily and intelligently cooperate for the common good. Humanists demand a shared life in a shared world.

Fifteenth and last: We assert that humanism will: (*a*) affirm life rather than deny it; (*b*) seek to elicit the possibilities of life, not flee from it; and (*c*) endeavor to establish the conditions of a satisfactory life for all, not merely for the few. By this positive *morale* and intention humanism will be guided, and from this perspective and alignment the techniques and efforts of humanism will flow.

So stand the theses of religious humanism. Though we consider the religious forms and ideas of our fathers no longer adequate, the quest for the good life is still the central task for mankind. Man is at last becoming aware that he alone is responsible for the realization of the world of his dreams, that he has within himself the power for its achievement. He must set intelligence and will to the task.

(signed)

J. A. C. Fagginger Auer—Parkman Professor of Church History and Theology, Harvard University; Professor of Church History, Tufts College.

E. Burdette Backus—Unitarian Minister.

Harry Elmer Barnes—General Editorial Department, Scripps-Howard Newspapers.

L. M. Birkhead—The Liberal Center, Kansas City, Missouri.

Raymond B. Bragg—Secretary, Western Unitarian Conference.

Edwin Arthur Burtt—Professor of Philosophy, Sage School of Philosophy, Cornell University.

Ernest Caldecott—Minister, First Unitarian Church, Los Angeles, California.

A. J. Carlson—Professor of Physiology, University of Chicago.

John Dewey—Columbia University.

Albert C. Dieffenbach—Formerly Editor of *The Christian Register.*

John H. Dietrich—Minister, First Unitarian Society, Minneapolis.

Bernard Fantus—Professor of Therapeutics, College of Medicine, University of Illinois.

William Floyd—Editor of *The Arbitrator,* New York City.

F. H. Hankins—Professor of Economics and Sociology, Smith College.

A. Eustace Haydon—Professor of History of Religions, University of Chicago.

Llewellyn Jones—Literary critic and author.

Robert Morss Lovett—Editor, *The New Republic;* Professor of English, University of Chicago.

Harold P. Marley—Minister, The Fellowship of Liberal Religion, Ann Arbor, Michigan.

R. Lester Mondale—Minister, Unitarian Church, Evanston, Illinois.

Charles Francis Potter—Leader and Founder, the First Humanist Society of New York, Inc.

John Herman Randall, Jr.—Department of Philosophy, Columbia University.

Curtis W. Reese—Dean, Abraham Lincoln Center, Chicago.

Oliver L. Reiser—Associate Professor of Philosophy, University of Pittsburgh.

Roy Wood Sellars—Professor of Philosophy, University of Michigan.

Clinton Lee Scott—Minister, Universalist Church, Peoria, Illinois.

Maynard Shipley—President, The Science League of America.

W. Frank Swift—Director, Boston Ethical Society.

V. T. Thayer—Educational Director, Ethical Culture Schools.

Eldred C. Vanderlaan—Leader of the Free Fellowship, Berkeley, California.

Joseph Walker—Attorney, Boston, Massachusetts.

Jacob J. Weinstein—Rabbi; Advisor to Jewish Students, Columbia University.

Frank S. C. Wicks—All Souls Unitarian Church, Indianapolis.

David Rhys Williams—Minister, Unitarian Church, Rochester, New York.

Edwin H. Wilson—Managing Editor, *The New Humanist*, Chicago, Illinois; Minister, Third Unitarian Church, Chicago, Illinois.

As associate editor of *The New Humanist* and initiator of the project, Raymond B. Bragg appended the manifesto with the following note, which has also appeared integrally to the manifesto in all successive editions:

> The Manifesto is a product of many minds. It was designed to represent a developing point of view, not a new creed. The individuals, whose signatures appear, would, had they been writing individual statements, have stated the propositions in differing terms. The importance of the document

is that more than thirty men have come to general agreement on matters of final concern and that these men are undoubtedly representative of a large number who are forging a new philosophy out of the materials of the modern world.

It is obvious that many others might have been asked to sign the Manifesto had not the lack of time and the shortage of clerical assistance limited our ability to communicate with them. The names of several who were asked do not appear. Reasons for their absence appear elsewhere in this issue of "The New Humanist." Further criticisms that we have been unable to publish have reached us; all of them we value. We invite an expression of opinion from others. To the extent possible "The New Humanist" will publish such materials.

Bragg's disclaimer was largely the result of correspondence with M. C. Otto and Arthur E. Morgan and is a reflection of Unitarian creedlessness. (Unfortunately, this appendage was inadvertently left out of the 1973 booklet published by Prometheus Books, which included *Humanist Manifesto I* [1933] and *Humanist Manifesto II* [1973].)

Continuing the policy of publishing divergent views, the same issue of *The New Humanist* in which the 1933 manifesto appeared also included the dissenting opinions of some nonsigners—Harold Buschman, John Haynes Holmes, Arthur E. Morgan, and Max C. Otto—whom we have already discussed.

In addition to drafting the initial text of "A Humanist Manifesto," we enlisted Roy Wood Sellars to write an interpretation of the document, which was also published in that issue of *The New Humanist* (VI:3:7–12). Entitled "Religious Humanism," this article was integral to the initial presentation of the manifesto. It follows here with only a few sentences deleted:

Religious Humanism

In the *Humanist Manifesto* it will be seen that many of us have reached a common body of beliefs and attitudes, beliefs about man, his place in the universe, the general nature of that universe, and attitudes toward the great questions of life. And we are certain that very many others, both in this country and abroad, have been thinking and feeling along these lines. Humanism offers to the world a set of new fundamentals on which to build personal and social life. These are the fundamentals as science, philosophy, and ethical insight are together grasping them, the fundamentals, I take it, of the age before us. Together they should furnish the basis for a valid and healthy reading of the nature, conditions, and possibilities of human living.

Now these humanist fundamentals are in many ways diametrically opposed to the fundamentals accepted by Christianity. I shall not attempt to answer the riddle, When is a Christian not a Christian? It reminds me, however, of the puzzle with which philosophers used to deal, the case of Sir John Suckling's stockings which were so much darned that none of the original silk remained in them. Were they still the original stockings? Not so long ago, the fundamentalist movement in the evangelical churches sought to get back to what they regarded as historical fundamentals. These were formulated in a very definite way and expressed, I think, the beliefs of the typical Protestant of a century ago. It would be another problem to determine how far they coincided with primitive Christianity or with the outlook of the Alexandrian fathers. But, in any case, the evangelical fundamentalists formulated a set of tenets which they regarded as true doctrine about man and the universe. I think that I can understand their motives for so doing and sympathize with at least some of them. It was with their appeal to the state to enforce their beliefs by legislation that I had no sympathy. It was natural; but could not succeed unless the trend was in their education. . . .

Under the influence of science and philosophy many churches and churchmen became liberal. They found it impossible to accept any longer the account of creation in Genesis and agreed that historical investigation had shown it to be a mixture of early Semitic myth and priestly theology. In like manner, miracles were doubted as contrary to the idea of immanent orderliness in the world. Here there was a touch of deism in liberalism. In short, the traditional theology was censored and toned down so that it lost its dramatic and concrete character. It was decided that the old views must be taken symbolically rather than literally.

The result of this liberalizing and deliteralizing was what is usually called modernism. But, in spite of its relinquishments of what is regarded as cruder beliefs, modernism, also, had its fundamentals. As nearly as I can judge, these consist of a belief in a regnant God, the validity of prayer and worship, and the acceptance of personal immortality. In the eyes of the modernist these constitute the minimum of religious fundamentals. I would say that he is doubtful that religion in any real sense of the word can survive the defeat of these fundamentals of his. He is quite certain that, beyond this minimum, Christianity ceases to exist. In relinquishing Jesus as the Son of God, Unitarianism had already stepped, to all intents and purposes, beyond the pale. Theism, I take it, is the basic fundamental of modernism.

And it is here that the battle is waging. To the consternation of the theist the humanist has arisen on the religious horizon to challenge his fundamentals and to assert that the time is ripe for a candid and impartial survey of the situation and its possibilities in the light of modern knowledge. Has the God-idea any longer a basis in the universe as we know it? And, if not, what becomes of the religious attitudes of prayer and worship dependent upon it? And, finally, what is the present standing of the notion of an after-life, a notion bound up with the traditional dualism between mind and body? Are these beliefs and the attitudes and activities integral with them capable of maintaining themselves when confronted by the thought of today? Such questions as these constitute the crisis of liberal Christianity. . . .

The question before us, then, is this, Are even the minimum theistic fundamentals tenable? The humanist says, No! He asserts that man must work out a new set of fundamentals and adjust his attitudes and expectations to them. Moreover, he maintains that these new fundamentals will be frankly naturalistic. Man is a child of nature, though a specially gifted child. . . . The psychological center of religion becomes for him intelligent forethought and purpose rather than petition and submission.

We may define religious humanism, accordingly, *as religion adjusted to an intelligent naturalism.* It is a religion in which man has become consciously the center of human thought and feeling. It is not a worship of an abstraction called humanity nor does it retain those traditional attitudes which are no longer relevant. It is religious because a concern for human values has always been the heart of religion. But it is a religion with a different perspective, a perspective based upon knowledge of man's situation rather than upon ignorance and imagination. . . .

We conclude that the humanist movement is a religious movement in that it is deeply concerned with the furtherance of human life along the lines indicated by reason and sympathetic intelligence. It is true that it represents a break with the traditional religious interpretation of life and the universe, but this is a sign of its vitality and novelty. If, as the humanist contends, the traditional religious interpretation of the world was illusory, the only manly thing to do is to acknowledge the mistake and make a fresh start. Man must interpret and direct his life, for this is inseparable from the very activity of living. Thought-frames and beliefs have always been secondary to this necessity. They are variables while this is a constant, as constant as life itself. If some prefer to speak of humanism as a philosophy of life, I would not be averse. But the careful students of comparative religions inform us that religion has always been one with the people's philosophy of life, with what they regarded as significant and imperative. The point is that the mists, fears, and hopes wrought of supernaturalism are vanishing. It is becoming daylight in the world. Man is at last beginning to understand himself and his situation, to know what he is "up against."

There remain two topics for consideration in this brief exposition of religious humanism: First, why the adoption of the term humanism? and, second, why the complete rejection of theism as a fundamental for the religion of our age and the ages that are coming?

We adopted the term humanism because it was, quite obviously, the one suitable term. Reject theism as the logical center of religion and the only alternative is to take man as the center. The new religion is homocentric and not theo-centric. Historians generally recognize that the passionate return to the literature and art of Greece, characteristic of the Renaissance, expressed in large part a turning away from the false asceticism and otherworldliness of much of the Middle Ages. I am not one of those who desire to paint too dark a picture of Medieval times; and yet I take it to be assured that there was this swing of human attention and interest. Literary humanism was part of a larger movement. Man felt more secure, more creative, more concerned with everyday affairs, with science, politics, trade, art.

And, recurrently since then, the term humanism has appeared to define this direction and concern. It was so used by Feuerbach and by Renan. The humanist was not a mere classicist but one who shared in the Greek sense of human values and dislike for the irrational and mystically authoritative. The humanist was one who took a joy in life and its possibilities and set his intelligence to work. Religious humanism is such humanism in the setting of modern science and philosophy. To narrow humanism to aesthetic classicism would be a crime. The religious humanist is not averse to a touch of romanticism to give vitality nor in his eyes is a pinch or two of humanitarianism and democracy an unmixed evil. All these can be mastered and used if the dominant spirit be that of fearless and intelligent deliberation upon the issues of human life. I must pass the consideration of literary humanism to the aesthetician and the literary critic.

And so we come at last to the question of the standing and the main characteristics of the naturalism which religious humanism accepts as a fundamental. Upon this I think all naturalists are agreed that between naturalism and theism it is a case of either-or. Either a reality corresponding to the God-idea is at the center of reality in a directing, planning way or there is no such reality. In the latter case, man is left to work out his own salvation as best he can with a fairly stable planet underneath his feet. His is the adventure and the goal.

It has always been my thesis that naturalism has today the logical priority. Nature is under observation in a way that God is not. It is difficult to put the contrast without paradox. For, of course, if God does not exist, he cannot be known. God does not exist means that the God-idea does not have application to what exists.

It is not my intention to brush aside all the arguments which have been used by Christians and other theists to show that the God-idea does have application. I must content myself with saying that none of these arguments have seemed to philosophers very convincing. As the support of traditional convictions is withdrawn, they become increasingly feeble. The one which seems to me most interesting goes back to Descartes and has appeared recently in new form as directed against the doctrine of emergent evolution. It is this, that the effect cannot be qualitatively different from the cause and the emergence of personality in the universe presupposes its prior existence. But to me, at least, this seems a dogma. Is it an *a priori* truth? How is it going to be validated as such? Novelty is a fact which runs all through nature with synthesis and organization. Naturalism studies nature to find out its pattern and what is, or is not, possible.

The naturalism which religious humanism accepts is not reductive. It takes man as he is with his gifts, with his mistakes and successes, in the scene, national and international, with which we are all becoming so familiar. Here lies man's job. Let him apply intelligence and a humane set of values to the business of living.

CHAPTER 14

Reactions from the Media

Concurrent to its appearance in *The New Humanist*, the manifesto was released to the media. Both Albert Dieffenbach of Boston and Charles Francis Potter of New York had expressed their willingness to help with publicity, and undoubtedly their expertise was useful. The press releases yielded some surprising results.

Herbert Yahraes, a religion editor for the Associated Press, wrote to Raymond Bragg on May 6, 1933, saying: "Many thanks for the 'Humanist Manifesto.' We used a story on it for Monday morning papers, May 1."

On May 1, 1933, John Evans, the religion editor of the *Chicago Tribune*, under the title, "Liberals See New Religion without God," summed up the manifesto's case:

> Inasmuch as a universe without God has no way of imparting "revelation," and because the inhabitants of a godless universe are devoid of "spirit," which is the vehicle of revelation's reception by mankind, then, in order to get on well in the universe, man must adopt a strictly scientific spirit, the humanist creed asserts. . . . Says the new creed: "Religion must formulate its hopes and plans in the light of the scientific spirit and method."

In spite of the manifesto's disclaimer of creedal intent, Evans dubbed it a creed. How quickly errors can creep into history! John Evans was also confused over the authorship of the manifesto—a misunderstanding we've already covered. Evans wrote: "Prof. Haydon added that he thought Prof. Sellers [*sic*] wrote the original draft and mailed it to prominent liberals of the country for review and amendment." But as we've discussed in previous chapters, it was Raymond Bragg who initiated the project and persuaded Roy Wood Sellars to write the first draft. It was principally Bragg and I who mailed it "to prominent liberals," and a committee of four (Bragg, Curtis Reese, A. Eustace Haydon, and myself) who edited it and incorporated numerous suggestions. No *one* person wrote "A Humanist Manifesto"; it was a consensus document.

The *Chicago Herald Examiner* also published a story on May 1, describing the manifesto as "a call for the establishment of a new religion" and listing the more prominent signatories. The article stated: "Proponents of the new code said that science and economic change have disrupted the old beliefs and that the time is ripe for coming to terms with new conditions created by a vastly increased knowledge and experience."

In New York City, an article in the May 1 *Herald Tribune* stressed the need to erase the distinction between *sacred* and *secular*, the affirmation that the universe is "self-existing and not created," and the revision of religious emotions as requirements of the manifesto. The *Herald Tribune* article also listed more than half of the thirty-four signatories.

The *Los Angeles Times* carried a full-column editorial, "The Faith of Our Fathers," which stated:

> Not only are these boosters of humanism in error in their main premise, that the religious forms and ideas of our fathers are no longer adequate for the needs of this age, but in their fifteen points they persistently put the secular before the sacred. . . .
>
> "Religions the world over," cry the humanists, "are under the necessity of coming to terms with new conditions." On the contrary, new conditions are under dire necessity of coming to terms with the religions of the world. Their failure to do so is illustrated in the miserable plight of the Russian workers, for whom, if the Soviets had not thrown over all reliance on the Divine, they might have been able to afford some relief.

And so began a heated "defense of the faith" (that is, theism) in the print media, which did not even wait for a response from religious leaders and the religious press. Not having had the benefits of a clipping service, I can only infer that many other papers dealt with the manifesto based upon the very spotty clippings I received from friends.

The Bristol, Connecticut, *Press* editorialized on May 19, 1933, referring to a report of the manifesto published in the same issue and ignoring the fact that over half of the thirty-four signatories were clerics. In fact, the paper chose to view college professors as being the "culprits" behind the manifesto:

> In another column of today's paper, appears a communication, quoting an article from the *Literary Digest*, signed by various and sundry college professors advocating a new religion, which these professors dub as "Humanism."
>
> Just as the day of the superbusiness man has passed, and it is realized that his advice in reference to business affairs is no better than that of the ordinary business man, so the day has also come when the college professor with his sophisticated pronouncement on all kinds of human affairs, should no longer be regarded as omniscient.
>
> College professors are much inclined to give out interviews on all sorts of human affairs. When, however, a mess of them such as have signed their names to this communication, show what they do not know about religion, we are reminded of an incident which happened in our college days, and which, we think, would be a first-rate cure to administer to these professors. This particular incident was known as, "Finlay's Conversion of Thomas." Finlay was a very ardent Episcopalian. Another member of the class had become very much interested in scientific study, and his investigations had led him to believe that everything in this universe came from cause to effect, without the directing hand of a supreme being in any way whatsoever. He was expressing his advanced ideas one Sunday afternoon. Finlay listened to what Thomas had to say, but he began to be considerably wrought-up, especially when Thomas denied the existence of a God.
>
> Finally Finlay could stand it no longer, and he stepped up to Thomas with these words: "Thomas, you say just

once more that there is no God, and I will knock Hell out
of you."

He meant exactly what he said for he was a strong
man. . . .

Such a dose of medicine is the only kind of argument
which these professors are capable of understanding and
in our humble opinion they would be cured.

Truly, the spirit of the Inquisition was not lacking even
in the early days of this century. In the name of the gentle
Jesus, doctrinaire Christians—even in 1933—were ready to
use violence to support their beliefs.

One of the most influential reports on "A Humanist Manifesto" was an article by Raube Walters, which included
an interview with sociologist F. H. Hankins, a professor at
Smith College and one of the signers. The article appeared
in the *Boston Evening Transcript*, for which Albert Dieffenbach, another manifesto signer, was the religion editor. Professor Hankins was quoted as saying:

The existence and being of God, the special and purpose-
ful creation of man, and the existence of the soul as a
separable entity are denied by the first three statements of
the fifteen propositions contained in this manifesto. As a
corollary to this is the elimination of any possibility of immortality. Humanism is realism in religion, the willing
destruction of illusions and delusions, and a willingness
to face facts with scientific precision. It destroys nothing
real and nothing which in the last analysis, is humanly
significant. . . .

In the same article, Raube Walters published statements
from three other signers—Albert Dieffenbach, Joseph Walker,
and J. A. C. F. Auer. Defining his position, Dr. Dieffenbach
was quoted:

I would not identify myself with anything that is attempted
to make an abrupt break with the past. Humanism is the
logical outcome of Christian thought. . . . Religion is still

religion though God in any conception of the word may
be disregarded. . . .

For my part I prefer not to abandon the word God,
for the reality in which I have my being, while it does not
correspond to the traditional theistic conception, is nevertheless the support of my life without which I could not
live in body, mind, or spirit. . . .

Obviously, Dieffenbach signed the manifesto despite differences with some of its tenets. That he did sign indicates his
agreement with the general spirit of the document.

Boston attorney Joseph Walker commented:

I signed the Humanist Manifesto because I am in general
accord with the statements therein contained. If men are
to discover a satisfactory way of life they must face squarely
the facts of life. Realistic thinking must take the place of
wishful thinking. Men may wish to believe in a personal
God, like the Christian God. Men may wish to believe in
a future life but the question is, not what men wish to
believe but rather what, with intellectual honesty, they can
believe. . . .

According to Raube Walters, J. A. C. F. Auer contended
that the manifesto contained both more and less than any of
the individuals signing it would have included and that, even
in the abridged form of its publication, stands in need of
rewriting. Dr. Auer was of the opinion that the manifesto
covered too much ground. According to Walters, Auer envi-
sioned humanism as a method of arriving at truth and did
not see in the phrasing of the first proposition any denial of
God. It was Auer's opinion that, if the humanists do so, they
are as much at fault as the theists in presuming to "know"
the truth.

In a sequel to his first article, this one entitled "In Re-
joinder to the Humanists, Five Theists Say Their Say," Walters
presented Catholic and Protestant reassertions of "their belief
in the Manifold Aspects of a Real God." One of those included was the Reverend James Luther Adams, then minister
of the Second Unitarian Church of Salem, Massachusetts,
and a distinguished theologian and authority on Paul Tillich

(another theologian). In a lengthy statement, Adams called the manifesto "in many respects irrelevant. . . . There is scarcely a signer of the Manifesto who is willing to defend all of its fifteen points." He dismissed the manifesto as "simply a journalistic venture intended for popular consumption." He denied that a violent controversy was raging in humanism and stressed the concern for free inquiry and improvement of the social order as shared by liberal theists and humanists.

The Roman Catholic perspective was offered by the Reverend Michael J. Ahern, then a radio commentator of the "Catholic Truth Hour" (broadcast on NBC from 1929 to 1956). Ahern stated:

> With the Manifesto of the Religious Humanists, a Catholic finds himself in some agreement. He would agree that any religion must recognize its obligations to a better social order; should work for a greater social justice for all men; cooperate for the common good of human life and human happiness; use its best endeavors to cultivate all the arts, all the sciences, all the culture and all the emoluments of civilization; in a word, bring to pass on earth, the greatest sum of genuine human happiness in a genuine human brotherhood. But the Catholic cannot agree that this implies that this universal goal can be attained by purely naturalistic or materialistic means.

A Protestant opinion was offered by the Reverend Russell Henry Stafford of the Old South Congregational Church at Copley Square in Boston. Dr. Stafford found the new movement "strangely named" and declared the name *humanism* had already been preempted by T. S. Eliot and Irving Babbitt —a preemption that history proved to be of short duration. Dr. Stafford held that "a modern philosophical theist will find much in the motivation of this movement [that is, the new form of humanism] with which to sympathize." He was referring to humanism's reaction to other-worldliness and the fact that "religious Humanism stands for the validity of moral idealism in its own right," as against "moral anarchy." He predicted that the new movement would have little viability because it is a "moderately interesting eccentricity, doctrinaire and impractical. . . . It is," Stafford declared, "a revamping of Auguste Comte's positivistic 'Religion of Humanity.' "

A fourth commentator in Walter's second *Transcript* article was the Reverend Dwight J. Bradley, a lecturer on worship at Newton-Andover Theological School in Massachusetts. He defended theism in terms of "experience"—a word that has done heavy duty in defense of the Christian faith in recent decades. "Intellectual theism is to my mind," said Bradley, "simply one way to try to define experience, either one's own or that of other men. . . . Theism is to me not an intellectual conception but a personal experience. A man is a theist because he's a mystic."

Here the issue of evidence is most certainly relevant. There is no question but that deep emotional experiences do occur, but there is a great probability of error in the interpretation of experience. Years later, inspired by Abraham Maslow, who spoke of "peak experiences and self-actualization," as well as by others, humanists were to find themselves studying the potentialities of naturalistic mysticism. The early issues of *Religious Humanism* explored the possibility of what George Santayana and others have called *naturalistic piety*, but I would venture to guess the average humanist holds that nothing short of adherence to scientific evidence can safeguard one against superstition. The question always is: what is the evidence? Humanists, relying upon the scientific method, usually would have a different sense of evidence than the theists. Humanists have a diminished will to believe that traditional symbols and doctrine correctly interpret experience. Furthermore, the theistic mystics usually articulate their experience in terms of their own cultural imagery and background.

Bradley summed up his position with a rather simplistic dismissal of the new movement, saying that "the general run of avowed religious Humanists are still suffering from a reaction against their early religious conditioning and early environment."

A dditional media reaction to the manifesto included comment by Dr. John Van Schaick, editor and manager of the *Christian Leader*, a Universalist publication (published prior to the merger with the Unitarians), who stated emphatically: "Here are men on the offensive. They are not in the church to be tolerated. They are in the church to make it over" (he might have said, "to humanize it"). He further stated:

> They have no apologies for the use of the word "religion." The time has come, they insist, to limit the use of the word to those processes that enrich life here and now. . . .
>
> These humanists do not want God and they will not have God. . . . Well, we are just as strong in our view. When we say God we mean God—omnipotent, omniscient, good, real, objective, personal, and super-personal, above us, beyond us, outside of us, inside of us, everywhere.

News of "A Humanist Manifesto" indirectly reached an important overseas newspaper thanks to Victor Moody, then Unitarian Minister at Horsham, England. In a July 24, 1933, letter to *The New Humanist*, Moody wrote:

> You may possibly be interested to see the enclosed letter, which I sent the other day to the *Manchester Guardian*. I did not, of course, mean to identify the New Humanism in any way with Irving Babbitt's, but as the notice of his death seemed to treat his work as the only humanism that the States knows, I thought it worth giving your recent Manifesto additional means of publicity, other than the more restricted one it received in our Unitarian paper, the "Inquirer," where, as no doubt you have seen, it created considerable discussion. Personally, I am delighted that you have been able to gather so many varying types of people on the same platform, and wish your work the greatest possible success. If you care to use the enclosed article in "The New Humanist" or elsewhere, please do so.
>
> I am, at the moment, busy finishing a book on Russia, which I recently visited, for Victor Gollancz, Ltd., London; when this is finished I hope to get in closer touch with your work, and would like, if possible, to get in a lecturing trip in the States some time next year.
>
> With best greetings from myself and other sympathetically-minded Britishers. . . .

Moody's appraisal of the humanist movement in America follows:

To the Editor of the Manchester Guardian:
Sir,—In your obituary notice of the late Prof. Irving Babbitt, the statement is made (apropos of the United States) that "to-day humanism is a dead topic." . . . This is by no means the case. Among the more thoughtful elements in the States, the humanist movement is making marked progress. More significantly still, it is becoming to-day less amorphous in its outlook, more sure of its philosophic grounds. It has restated its position in terms less nebulous, and more definitely in keeping with the swift trends of economic and historical thought. It is thus gaining power as a dynamic weapon of social and political change, the importance of which it would be foolish to underestimate.

As evidence of this, it is sufficient to call attention to a recent Manifesto, published in the May-June issue of "The New Humanist" (Chicago) in which is outlined a constructive programme—both religious and political—of a drastic nature and of comprehensive scope. It is particularly significant that this Manifesto has succeeded in uniting on one common platform, influential citizens of widely differing types, men like Prof. John Dewey and Rabbi Jacob Weinstein (Columbia University), Prof. J. A. C. F. Auer (Church History, Harvard University), and Laymen like Harry Elmer Barnes (of the Editorial Board of the Scripps-Howard Newspapers). Its other signatories include, besides other University and religious leaders, editors and journalists, the names of well-known scientists, medical men, economists, sociologists, and lawyers. In view of the radical nature of the Manifesto, particularly in its economic aspects (as in [section fourteen]), the influential support already given to it from so many representative quarters at leasts suggests that, so far from being "a dead topic," Humanism in the United States is very much alive. . . .

Moving more slowly than the newspapers, magazines soon began to deal with "A Humanist Manifesto." Most of these commentaries were less than friendly and objective.

Like a voice from the past, the *Literary Digest*, under

the heading "For a New Religion—Humanism" (May 20, 1933) stated:

> A New Religion for a new day is the cry of thirty-four editors, educators and ministers.
>
> It is humanism they demand, to which all the old forms of piety, prayer and belief must give way.
>
> Let the supernatural go; abandon the hope learned in Sunday-school and at mother's knee. Let science rule the conscience; let men work together for the common good.
>
> So, in short, say these teachers of youth who met recently in Chicago and issued a statement urging the establishment of a religion "shaped for the needs of this age" because "the religious forms and ideas of our fathers are no longer adequate."
>
> Easter Day was not far behind when this statement was issued, and the tens of thousands who attended dawn services on the Resurrection morn may be sufficient to show that the creedless creed has not many converts yet.
>
> The humanism offered by the thirty-four—nearly three times the number of those first to spread the Gospel—is explained thus, according to the Associated Press: . . .

Following ten direct quotes from the manifesto, the article continued:

> If none of the present religions suits modern requirements, observed the *Columbus Ohio State Journal*, there are no obstacles to developing a new one. Which might help those who have none now. And this paper recalls:
>
>> Roland Hill once remarked, "I would give nothing for that man's religion whose very dog and cat were not the better for it."
>>
>> This appeals to us as a very good yardstick. We suggest when the Chicago group gets its new-fangled religion in shape it try it out on the cat.

The article concluded by listing a selection of the signers.

The May 15, 1933, issue of *Time* magazine dealt with the manifesto in similar fashion but with less bias, and it wrongly stated that "more and more humanists are to read the manifesto, sign it, make suggestions, which may perhaps be incorporated. . . ." Further signers were not sought, nor was it ever out intention to seek them. *Time* was correct, however, about suggestions being encouraged. The article began:

> Humanism used to be a good subject for parlor and dinner table discussions. Few people knew what it actually was, or where literary Humanism left off and religious Humanism began. Nor did Humanism's expounders get together and codify their beliefs for popular enlightenment. Rev. Charles Francis Potter, one time Baptist, Unitarian and Universalist, hired Steinway Hall in Manhattan (*Time*, Oct. 21, 1929) and still preaches therein, but Professor Irving Babbitt taught something different, and Dr. Paul Elmer More on religious grounds denied them both.
>
> Last week, for the first time, the religious Humanists were on common ground. After discussing many questions (by letter) they had drawn up, signed and circulated a manifesto containing their articles of faith. More and more Humanists are to read the manifesto, sign it, make suggestions which may perhaps be incorporated after due consideration. Vague as it still may be, Humanism may now be said to stand as follows:
>
> • The universe is self-existing, not created.
> • Man is part of nature, product of his culture, his environment, his social heritage. The traditional dualism of mind and body must be rejected.
> • Humanism also rejects cosmic and supernatural "guarantees." The Humanist eschews theism, deism, modernism, "new thought" and instead of feeling religious emotions concentrates on human life—labor, art, science, philosophy, love, friendship, recreation.
> • Humanism is for "a socialized and cooperative economic order—a shared life in a shared world. . . ."
>
> Most Humanists come from Unitarian, Universalist, Baptist and Congregational churches. In recent years 60 Unitarian ministers have embraced Humanism. Their church was dismayed but could do nothing, its own creed being far from stringent. There are Humanist groups in Manhattan, Hollywood, Berkeley, Calif., Sioux City and Minneapolis. . . .

The article concluded by listing signers Potter, Barnes, Dewey, Dieffenbach, Lovett, Shipley, Walker, and "26 others."

The *Standard*, back in 1933, was the monthly periodical of the American Ethical Union and was served by George E. O'Dell as managing editor and an editorial board of nine. (It wasn't until 1952 that the AEU aligned itself with humanism by helping to form the International Humanist and Ethical Union.) One of the board members, Algernon Black, wrote in the May 1933 *Standard:*

> From *The New Humanist* comes an advance copy of an item entitled ["A Humanist Manifesto"]. It is signed chiefly by liberal ministers, but includes also a number of important college professors, and two names (Dr. V. T. Thayer and Mr. W. Frank Swift) identified . . . with the Ethical Movement. The purpose of the manifesto is to describe a humanist religion. The signatories commit themselves, in the course of a considerable series of propositions, to statements asserting that the universe is self-existent and not created, that the traditional dualism of mind and body must be rejected, that there can be no cosmic guarantees of human values, that the time has passed for theism, and— turning to practical matters—that the present acquisitive and profit-motivated society must be radically changed, and that "the goal of humanism is a free and universal society in which people voluntarily and intelligently cooperate for the common good."
>
> Purposely we have included above some of the most controversial of the items. Many members of Ethical Societies will no doubt accept them all. And unquestionably— for all that the new *Year Book of the Churches* (Round Table Press, New York) declares such humanism to be dying— these tenets can belong in an entirely creditable religion. But obviously it cannot be the official religion of an Ethical Society, any more than can Utilitarianism, or the august ethical metaphysics of our late Leader, Dr. Adler. Indeed, could anything better help us to urge the rightness of the kind of fellowship sought to be established by our societies? For we do not as societies seek to make that deeply serious regard for the cultivation of better human relations, for greater justice, truthfulness, sympathy, tolerance,

disinterestedness, which we feel to be religious *depend* on any doctrine such as those quoted above.

That persons should be encouraged by us to seek honest and intelligent views about body-mind psychology, theism (in its modern innumerable varieties), the ultimate nature of matter and force, what not, let us all agree. But there must be room in our fellowship on equal terms of respect and service for those to whom the garnered moral experience of mankind at its best and most forward-looking, demands supreme allegiance, whether the cosmos favors it or not, and whether there is a supersensible reality or not. Every newly-labelled religion, even humanism, while legitimate in its place, is, alas, liable to be a new means of intellectualist separatism. The only separation the Ethical Movement acknowledges as inevitable to it is that between those to whom the life of moral obligation is fundamental on its own account, and those to whom it is not.

In the London *Inquirer* for June 3, 1933, Edwin Fairley, a Unitarian minister, then the regular American correspondent of the British Unitarians, reported:

The lastest number of *The New Humanist* contains a Humanist Manifesto signed by a large number of clergymen and others which sets forth some fifteen theses which these men are willing to sign. Fifteen of the signers are Unitarian clergymen, and the others are members of the Universalists, Ethical Culture Society, or laymen. The thesis which will provoke most comment is the sixth which declares, "We are convinced that the time has passed for theism, deism, modernism, and the several varieties of 'new thought.'" Some men who are usually classed among the humanists have not signed the Manifesto, among them Dr. Harold Buschman, editor of *The New Humanist*, and John Haynes Holmes who, though calling himself a Humanist, is unwilling to sign what looks like a creed.

The *Christian Register*, then the official publication of the American Unitarian Association, published on May 25, 1933, the *Boston Transcript* article in its entirety under the title "Comments by Some Who Signed" along with additional statements entitled "Comments by Some Who Did Not Sign."

Within the latter article, the *Register* reprinted the statements by Harold Buschman, John Haynes Holmes, and M. C. Otto which had appeared along with the manifesto in *The New Humanist*.

Interestingly, though not surprising given the high level of participation of Unitarians in the humanist movement, the former editor of the *Register*, Albert Dieffenbach, had signed the manifesto, as did its future editor, Llewellyn Jones, who edited the periodical for three years beginning in 1938.

Unity magazine, published in Chicago by the Western Unitarian Conference (and not to be confused with the Kansas City *Unity*), simply printed the entire manifesto as well as the criticism of it from the same issue of *The New Humanist*. Curiously, there was no editorializing in the *Unity* report, which may have been due to the fact that Holmes and Curtis Reese were functioning uneasily as coeditors (the two differed on religious issues as well as American foreign policy). Holmes ultimately resigned and Reese became sole editor.

There must have been many more reactions in religious periodicals. *Christianity Today* raised one continuous wail for years over the "threat" of humanism. But the most notable comments are to be found in the June 7, 1933, issue of the *Christian Century* (the Chicago-based weekly which identified itself as "An Undenominational Journal of Religion"). Reports at the time from the University of Chicago campus were that an editor had to work all night to tone down the original article, written by Dr. Charles Clayton Morrison, in order that the emotional attack which allegedly bore the marks of a temper tantrum might not demean a usually liberal and tolerant publication. Over two full pages were given to the unsigned editorial:

> A contemporary group which likes to be known as "humanists" is rendering distinct service to the cause of theism. Their statements lend themselves as a kind of foil against which modern enlightened theism finds it more or less convenient to state its own case. The group has recently

published a "Manifesto," consisting of fifteen articles in which are set forth the major theses of a "religion without God." It deserves to be exhibited in theistic as well as anti-theistic circles. The *Christian Century* frankly admits that it is unable to deal with the document in the spirit of calm respect which we would like to accord to certain of its signatories. These include certain writers, college professors and leftwing Unitarian ministers for whom even the liberal Unitarian faith is intolerably orthodox.

After listing all thirty-four signatories (without their professional identification), the editorial continued:

The manifesto is an astonishing exhibition of irrelevant and immature statements touching philosophical subjects. The reader is compelled to rub his eyes as he scans the names of the signatories, and particularly as he finds there the name of Professor John Dewey. That America's most influential philosopher could have shared in the writing of these theses, or that he could have seriously intended his subscription to approve them as a philosophical basis for a new religion, is incredible. We desire to set the document before our readers, and to add a brief comment upon each article.

The editorial then proceeded to summarize all fourteen points with criticism that can be recognized as competent apologetics (defense of the faith). For example, point one: ". . . this concept does not imply a dualism between the Creator and the Universe, but rather a conception of the universe which includes the creative process as inherent." Point two: theists and humanists can agree that man is part of nature but, writes this critic, " 'nature' will have to make a place for much that, in the older framework, was called 'supernatural.' " I won't comment on the *Christian Century*'s treatment of each point; however, I will say that, forensically, one often attempts to dismiss a point by sarcasm. For example, following point six, "We are convinced that the time has passed for theism, deism, modernism, and the several varieties of 'new thought,' " the editorial commented: " '*We* are convinced' that this sentence was lifted bodily from some sophomore's term paper." In response to point seven, "Religion consists of those actions, purposes, and experiences which are humanly significant . . ." it reads, "True, and fairly well spoken. The humanists learned this from theists." The *Century* offers this commentary on the manifesto's ninth point, "No more worship and prayer but 'a heightened sense of personal life.' That is an honest and pertinent distinction. It designates accurately the only proper emotion of which a 'religion' is capable which begins and ends with 'man.' . . ."

It is in the concluding remarks of the editorial that we have the ultimate confrontation between the editors of the *Christian Century* and the signers of "A Humanist Manifesto." Three long, critical paragraphs begin with:

> "Man is at last becoming aware," etc. This statement we deny. . . .We affirm that the thing of which man is becoming aware is that he *alone* is *not* responsible for such realization. He has been trying all too long to realize his dreams as if he were alone responsible. His man-made social order has broken down because he has taken no account of his cosmic Partner in this great business, and as he surveys the wreck of his efforts, he is just beginning to awaken to the fact that there exists in the universe beyond his egoistic, humanistic self, a living Power, or Process, or Something. . . .

Toward the end of these paragraphs some *ad hominem* remarks appear, perhaps a sample of the sort of thing that the editor reportedly weeded out:

> . . . The elementary fallacy of the sort of humanism revealed in this "manifesto" lies in its sophomoric and philosophically meaningless asseveration that man "has within himself the power" for the achievement of the world of his dreams. It tears "man" out of the context of nature and bloats him with unconscionable egoism or reduces him to despair.

The force of this criticism has come home to more than one humanist writer in the years since 1933, but as humanists they still do not look for cosmic or supernatural guarantees of survival. Instead they have faith that humankind has a chance if we all will draw upon the forces of good will and skill inherent in our makeup. In the words of an inscription said to be emblazoned over a cooperative warehouse: humankind must "Cooperate or Die."

The final paragraph of the *Century* editorial attempts to speak for John Dewey, but I believe it is off target:

> The humanists may call this by the name "religion" if they wish to, but they have no business to call it philosophy, despite the fact that certain well-known teachers of philosophy grace the "manifesto" with their signatures. We have no right to make any statement concerning any of the signatories save one. That one is Professor Dewey. It is unbelievable that his signature was intended to underwrite the whole of this document. Philosophically, it moves in a different realm from that which Mr. Dewey's own interpretation of nature and experience has opened up to the modern mind. It represents an emphasis which he does not make, and its major thesis of the sufficiency of man to achieve his goals by himself alone, and by resources which are within himself alone, is contradictory of the whole trend of Mr. Dewey's thought.

I have said very little up to this point about John Dewey and the significance of his signature on the 1933 manifesto. Certainly, he was the most famous of all the signers. As noted previously, Dr. Dewey appended his name to the draft manifesto with no further comment.

On August 30, 1940, Corliss Lamont, at that time an active humanist and director of the American Civil Liberties Union, sent John Dewey a letter. (The next year, Lamont would join the board of directors for the newly founded American Humanist Association, whose organizational voice was *The Humanist*, successor to *The New Humanist*.) Dewey and Lamont had been correspondents since 1935, following the publication of Dewey's *A Common Faith*. In this letter, Lamont wrote:

Since in 1933 you signed the Humanist Manifesto . . . I

am wondering why you have not used the word "Humanism" more to describe your own philosophy. Though I realize this term "Humanism" is open to misconception, it is certainly far less formidable for the average person, whom you wish philosophy to reach, than the term Pragmatism or Instrumentalism or even Naturalism. And of course these latter words have also given rise to plenty of misunderstanding.

A week later, on September 6, Dewey replied, explaining why he signed the manifesto:

There is a great difference between different kinds of "Humanism" as you know; there is that of Paul Elmer More for example. I signed the humanist manifesto precisely because of the point to which you seem to object, namely because it had a religious context, and my signature was a sign of sympathy on that score, and not a commitment to every clause in it.

"Humanism" as a technical philosophic term is associated with [F. C. S.] Schiller and while I have great regard for his writings, it seems to me that he gave Humanism an unduly subjectivistic turn—he was so interested in bringing out the elements of human desire and purpose neglected in traditional philosophy that he tends it seems to me to a virtual isolation of man from the rest of nature. I have come to think of my own position as cultural or humanistic Naturalism—Naturalism, properly interpreted seems to me a more adequate term than Humanism. Of course I have always limited my use of "instrumentalism" to my theory of thinking and knowledge; the word pragmatism I have used very little, and then with reserves.

While John Dewey clearly preferred the term *naturalism* as it applied to his philosophy, he was for years an active supporter of several humanist organizations. From 1933 until his death in 1952, he served on the advisory board of the First Humanist Society of New York, organized by Charles Potter. Since its inception in 1941, Dewey was a member of and financial contributor to the American Humanist Association, and he wrote the occasional article for *The Humanist*. The

AHA honored him by naming one of its most prestigious awards after him. I am very proud to have been among his correspondents.

Chapter 15

Responses from Individuals

C omments on the manifesto received from individuals after publication were important to us because part of the motivation behind publishing the manifesto was to catalyze discussion and promote the development of humanism.

Edgar S. Brightman

One valued letter came from Edgar S. Brightman, who was then teaching in the philosophy department of the Graduate School of Boston University (he also taught at Boston University's School of Theology). Brightman wrote:

> The "Humanist Manifesto" is really worth while. Any clarification of the air is valuable. As a theist, I find myself in disagreement only with the fifth and sixth points (and the ninth and tenth, which follow from them). The others seem to me to be full of evidence for theism! I wonder whether the last sentence of the fifth point means a repudiation of philosophy in favor of science, in which case I wonder where loyalty to values comes in. From the eleventh on, I am heartily in agreement.

Although I never met Professor Brightman personally, we kept in touch; he sent critical comments, pro and con articles, and reviews which I published after 1941 as editor of *The Humanist.* A friendly liberal theist voice such as Brightman's was invaluable and functioned within a framework of cooperative coexistence which today's extreme fundamentalists probably would not understand; but it's a good idea for humanists to work with liberal theists for shared goals. Dr. Brightman was primarily a teacher, encouraging critical thought on religion wherever he found it.

Edward S. Boyer

Comments on the manifesto by E. S. Boyer, professor of religion at James Millikin University in Decatur, Illinois, were published in the July/August 1933 issue of *The New Humanist* (VI:4:47); "A Humanist Manifesto" had appeared in the previous issue. Boyer wrote:

> I believe the "Humanist Manifesto" to be one of the most brave and courageous attempts at clearing away the debris in the religious field that has been made for a century. There is every evidence of the acme of religious goals being stated. Therein may lie its difficulty. Intellectualization is the basic work. The machinery is all there except important parts of the dynamo.
>
> Social living down at its "grass roots" has powerful urges that drive the human life into fierce group action. The pilgrimage of life for any alert individual is full of such phases. Controls issuing from an intellectualized credo can only be partially successful in guiding toward commonly desired ethicised human conduct. Emotional tides whence come fervor, zeal, and, abandon of life for a cause, overflow reinforced dykes, still flow through society. That some such tides lay waste and do much destruction, none can deny. But that others function to cleanse and clarify must also be admitted. The fact that we must account for such each day in the realm of politics, economics and common social action is proof positive of its presence. The "battle and the march" seem to require it. How compose the difficulties that issue from the heat of such dynamic human action? The live currents and cross-currents arising from the intermingling of the passions of love, hate,

loyalty and established prejudices must be guided to higher levels through emotional attachment to living reality as well as to living thought.

My sincere desire would be to say that the "Manifesto" is sufficient for these things. Truly speaking, I fear it will not be. It seems confined to a selected corner of life but aloof from the total field of humanity's life and death struggle. There will be stiff criticism at this point. I hope and believe that such criticism will not vitiate the good work and noble spirit of the thirty-four men who signed this significant and history-making document. Nor will the rest of us who believe so largely with them, be deterred from stronger efforts at establishing rational and scientific norms for developing spiritual fruit borne of common intelligent action through personalizing qualities of the good life.

E. J. Unruh

E. J. Unruh, then minister of the Central Universalist Church in Indianapolis, wrote a letter on May 9, 1933, to Harold Buschman, editor of *The New Humanist*. Buschman scribbled a candid note to his staff: "This is just jibberish!—Poorly written, in any case. Too much near-rhetoric." Too long to print as a whole, two paragraphs from Unruh's letter should suffice to reflect his point of view:

> . . . The Manifesto fails to state why I *want* to be a humanist. What moves me to forsake the traditional affirmations, launch out into the dangers of uncertainties, and constrains me to desire to spend myself in the interest of man? There seems to be a sort of motivating influence that is within and of the self, yet it is above the self. It is not what the traditionalist calls God but it is what I should very much like to call God. . . .
>
> A description of my religious self must include a joyful recognition of all integrating influences and the repulsiveness of disintegrating influences, an appreciation of the life-giving and motivating forces and also a positive disapproval of the life-taking and negating forces. . . .

In spite of all this and above all this I am constrained to maintain that I am a humanist but not such a one as is described by the manifesto. . . .

I have greatly enjoyed the May-June issue of *The New Humanist*. Here is the subscription price.

George R. Dodson

Dr. George R. Dodson, a scholarly critic of the views espoused by Reese and Dietrich well before the publication of the manifesto, submitted an article, "What the Manifesto Lacks," which was published in the September/October 1933 issue of *The New Humanist* (VI:5:28–32):

> Notwithstanding my great respect for the names signed to the Humanist Manifesto and my enthusiastic agreement with some of its affirmations—for example numbers 2, 8, 12, 13, and 15—I cannot escape the conviction that the declaration is, if not hasty, at least not sufficiently considered. It is defective and erroneous in several important respects of which I desire to indicate a few.
>
> First, then, it ignores the fact that some of its affirmations, for example those I have mentioned, have been and are being enthusiastically made by theistic and modernistic churches for which the Manifesto declares there is no longer any place. What is announced as something new and revolutionary is familiar to many thinkers and practical workers in the religious field. It is a fact that a very large percentage of the movements for philanthropy, charity, social reform, education and enlightenment have been initiated and led by liberal church people, the immense majority of whom are theists. This is not the place to confirm this statement by giving a list of the many progressive movements started and developed by men and women who never dreamed that there was anything incompatible between their theism and humanism. Indeed, their theistic religion has tremendously reinforced their humanistic efforts, for they have deeply felt that in their humanitarian efforts they were working not against the main currents of life in the world, but that they were themselves

organs of creative intelligence, of upward tendencies in the universe.

Second, the many men and women who have spent themselves and their resources in the endeavor to better existing conditions have meant by religion not what the Manifesto means by it, but what the great majority of religious men and women have always understood and still understand by the term. The Manifesto defines religion as the quest for the good life; but I do not think that philosophers of religion generally would define religion in this way —for this quest may be pursued with or without religion. The proponents of the Manifesto are defining religion in a way in which it has almost never been defined. Surely the consensus of enlightened opinion is that men pursue the quest for the good life religiously when they believe or trust or hope that the cosmos is favorable to their idealistic efforts, that we live in a world in which our ideals can be realized and that in our intellectual, ethical, and aesthetic enthusiasms we work with, and not against, the personality-producing forces of the universe. Notwithstanding the diversity of religious doctrines, on one essential point there is general agreement. It has been stated by Paulsen with great clearness as follows:

"For in truth the real essence of every religious belief is the assurance that the true nature of reality reveals itself in that which I love and reverence as the highest and the best; it is the certainty that the good and perfect, towards which the deepest yearning of my will is directed, forms the origin and the goal of all things." . . .

This characteristic of essential religion is ignored in the definition adopted by the Manifesto. It declares that theism is obsolete, that the time for it has passed, that henceforth we are definitely through with the idea of God. Humanism is thus either anti-theistic or it treats the great idea with studied indifference. . . . There are even people who think they are not religious but who teach their children that the way to the highest values is lighted by the ideals of truth, beauty, and goodness. But to say this is to say a great deal about the universe, for it is implicitly to affirm that the universe is of such a nature that the highest, the most satisfactory and blessed life will be enjoyed by those whose lives are consecrated to the realization of intellectual, aesthetic, and social ideals. But that is theism, and the Manifesto mentions it only to dismiss it summarily and unceremoniously. It would have been well for the Manifesto to be clear about the theism which it rejects—for there are three possibilities: (a) that reality is sub-human, (b) that it is precisely human (anthropomorphic), (c) that it is superpersonal and that we are justified in our use of personal symbols because, though inadequate, they are the highest that we have. They mean too little and not too much. . . .

Religion is, then, a triumphant attitude of the spirit of man. It can never be a matter of demonstration in the scientific sense and it does not have to ask of science permission to be. . . .

Roy Wood Sellars

Continuing its tradition of civilized dialogue—and having welcomed a competent critic in the spirit of Dr. Haydon's oft-repeated dictum: "A movement should be judged by its best exemplars"—Professor Roy Wood Sellars was asked to respond to the published manifesto. In the November/December 1933 issue of *The New Humanist* (VI:6:6–12), his article, "In Defense of the Manifesto," referred to a previous controversy he had had with Dr. Dodson:

> It was with considerable interest that I read Professor Dodson's critique of the Humanist Manifesto. I could anticipate in some measure his general reaction to the perspective in religious matters represented by the Manifesto and his probable rejection of certain of the theses, and this because I knew his position in philosophy, having had, as a matter of fact, a slight controversy with him on the subject of naturalism a few years ago. It would, in fact, have surprised me if he had agreed with the obviously naturalistic point of view of the declaration of principles offered to the public as a basis for discussion.
>
> And that is just what a manifesto is. It is a public declaration of principles giving reasons and grounds. It presents something to be debated, something which its

proponents are ready to defend to the best of their ability because they have a sincere belief in what it stands for. There is no suggestion of the authoritarian about it. It follows that all who sign are ready to welcome vigorous criticism. There can be no hesitation about so classing Dr. Dodson's article.

The Manifesto must, I think, be taken as a whole. It presents fifteen theses which together express a standpoint which is at one and the same time naturalistic and humanistic. Herein lies its novelty. . . . Man is a child of Nature, and yet with unique and distinctive abilities and needs. By his intelligence and wisdom he must, if possible, guide his life and use it creatively. It is my impression that Dr. Dodson does not fully realize the crucial importance for the whole Manifesto of this encompassing perspective. The various theses are but arguments of it or corollaries. Their unity comes from it. . . .

I would point out that we did not regard it as our job at the time to compare and contrast our position with other positions. We knew that would be done in the discussion that followed. We were concerned primarily with the development of the assumptions, objectives, and motivations of a naturalistic humanism. It did not occur to us to deny that there had lived all sorts of noble men in the past or that humanitarianism was widespread among liberal people. . . . We conceived humanism as a perspective which would give vigor and rigor to ethical thinking and not as something which would miraculously introduce the milk of human kindness where it was lacking.

And this brings me to another point. Naturalistic humanism offers itself as an outlook expressive of the world-view and the philosophy of human life which is growing up all over the world among educated and reflective people. In this sense, it regards itself as a possible world-religion correspondent to the coming unification of world-culture. Just as the scientific interpretation of the world is being accepted today in Tokio [*sic*] and Calcutta and Peking [*sic*] as well as in London, Paris, Chicago and Moscow, so it may well be that, in the years to come, a somewhat analogous philosophy of human life will arise in connection with it.

I hope, then, that rationalists, Confucians, Marxists, Hindus, Unitarians, Episcopalians, Baptists, etc. will feel somewhat as Dr. Dodson does about the Manifesto, namely, that its ethical outlook is not altogether alien to theirs but that, taken as a whole, it represents a stimulating and really novel perspective. . . .

Although the final product of "A Humanist Manifesto" was the work of many contributors, Dr. Sellars' influence ought not to be underrated. He was a philosopher of national prestige and, according to *The Encyclopedia of Philosophy,* "Sellars has maintained a substantial reputation . . . as a vigorously independent thinker. His thought is rigorous and critical, he has never yielded to the fashionable movements of the day but has steadfastly pursued his own original insights into basic . . . problems."

Archie J. Bahm

Yet another person who identified with organized humanism almost since its inception was Archie J. Bahm. Later a professor of philosophy at the University of New Mexico, at the time he wrote the following letter, he was a Teaching Fellow in philosophy at the University of Michigan, where he obtained his doctorate. Bahm wrote to Buschman at *The New Humanist* on May 17, 1933:

> A copy of "The New Humanist," containing "A Humanist Manifesto," has just come to my hands. The manifesto reminds me of a "religious creed" which I wrote some time ago, and which won first place in contest conducted by the Liberal Students Union (Unitarian)—a contest in which all University of Michigan students were eligible to compete. I submit it to you, hoping that you may find it to be of some use.
>
>   The judges of the contest were Professor Roy Wood Sellars, of the Department of Philosophy, Professor John F. Shepard, of the Department of Psychology, and Professor Robert C. Angell, of the Department of Sociology—all of the University of Michigan.

There followed Bahm's "A Religious Affirmation," which we

published in the July/August issue of *The New Humanist:*

A Religious Affirmation

A man should—

1. Be creedless; that is, be intelligent enough to make adaptations without dependence upon some formula.
2. Be self-reliant; that is, be not dependent upon supernatural agency for intellectual support or moral guidance.
3. Be critical; that is, question assumptions and seek certitude scientifically.
4. Be tolerant; that is, be openminded and hold conclusions tentatively.
5. Be active; that is, live today and grow by exercising his capacities.
6. Be efficient; that is, accomplish the most with the least effort.
7. Be versatile; that is, vary his interests to attain a variety of interesting thoughts.
8. Be cooperative; that is, find some of his satisfactions in social activities.
9. Be appreciative; that is, make the present enjoyable by his attitude.
10. Be idealistic; that is, create and live by ideals which he finds inspiring.

I think this affirmation demonstrates something I have often noticed—that is, different schools of philosophy arrive religiously and ethically at humanism.

John H. Hershey

John H. Hershey, then minister of the Unitarian Church in Laconia, New Hampshire, wrote to *The New Humanist* largely in defense of the continued use of God-language, but in a cosmic sense, as shown by these quotes from his letter:

There can be no doubt that the "Manifesto" distinctly opposes the idea of a personal, supernatural being, judging from numerous passages. But it should be said emphatically that the idea of God thus opposed is not the only idea of God. There are other ideas of God which may be reasonable, even if the supernatural idea is not.

Another idea which has been held in the past and is held today is that of God as the eternal principle of order in the universe. God, so thought of, did not create the universe at one time, but is eternally transforming it. Man was not miraculously created, but naturally sprang from the earth. The cause and effect processes of nature are the workings of the eternal principle we call God. Indeed, the organic view of human nature, of man and nature, and of all nature makes rational the idea of one unifying principle of all things, and this principle is God. For it is difficult, logically, to have an organic view of man and nature without an immanent, unifying principle. Now, with this idea of God in mind, instead of a personal, supernatural deity, let us consider some of the statements of the "Manifesto."

It states, for example, that the universe is self-existing, that man is a part of nature and has emerged as the result of a continuous process, that the traditional dualism of mind and body must be rejected for an organic view, and that culture and civilization are products of a gradual development. Furthermore, the possibility of realities not as yet discovered is not denied. These statements are opposed to the idea of a personal, supernatural deity. But are they opposed to the idea of God as eternal and immanent unity? No! In fact, they are necessary for a belief in divine immanence.

Albert Dieffenbach

I have previously pointed out that, at the time the manifesto was published, Albert Dieffenbach had become the religion editor for the *Boston Evening Transcript*. The following essay by Dieffenbach reads like an editorial, but when Raymond Bragg turned it over to me after finding it in his files, there was no indication that it had ever been published.

Here is a sincere effort to state what a body of earnest thinkers believe is the religion of the new era. Though the humanist manifesto takes the form of a precise definition of faith, it is much more an earnest expression of principles by which people live out their lives in a growing world. Every one of the signers is a religious person, bringing the intelligence directly to bear upon truth for life, and keeping all of the other factors which must be present in a complete religion. As Carlyle said of his father, these men are religious with the consent of all their faculties. I know there are tens of thousands of persons who are ready for the manifesto and will accept it with spiritual satisfactions. Today we are undergoing revolutionary changes in all of our ways of thinking, political, social, and economic, and it is a simple fact that people are not at all alarmed or disturbed by the casting off of the old order for the new and better time. Religion, which really embraces all of the elements of our life into one binding unity, is of course under obligation to restate its fundamentals. That is what make this body of universal essentials of paramount importance in our present evolution to a higher order of personal and corporate life throughout the world.

It will please the careful reader that the manifesto is affirmative and optimistic. While there is a becoming unwillingness to make dogmatic assertions about certain things which we do not know, there is also an inspiring and forward-marching faith in what is known and accepted by all good men. There is nothing lacking in the manifesto to make a religion of infinite power and glory for this present world. The most devoted follower of any one of the world's great religions will find here the ultimate ideas and ideals which have moved the race onward. For it is simple truth that every religion is at last humanistic. That is, the great faiths have all had human leaders who were conceived as prophets or divinities. The power of these religions has come from the human attributes which have been sublimated and united in religion. When men say, for example, God is love, they form a concept of the holiest quality in the human heart. And so with every other element in religion of every variety, throughout the ages. All are ours. In men are the potential religious talents, and to perfect him in character and to supply him with a dynamic for service to humanity, is the whole duty of religion and the peculiar obligation for us of this age of liberation in the truth and of advancement of the rights, the goodness, and the happiness of mankind.

W. Frank Swift

W. Frank Swift was a classmate of Raymond Bragg's at theological school and a leader for a brief time of the St. Louis Ethical Society. Swift was among the younger generation of signers of the manifesto:

> It becomes apparent that institutionalized religion is losing its effectiveness as a social force in the modern world. This loss of effectiveness is largely due to the fact that the churches have become marooned on an island of theological ideas and practices. . . . It is in emphasizing the fact of human responsibility for achieving the goal of the quest for the good life that humanist religion finds its prophetic function in the modern world.

Swift died in an automobile accident in December 1933 at the age of thirty-two.

W. Hanson Pulsford

A letter came to Raymond Bragg from the Reverend W. Hanson Pulsford, which has particular poignancy because Pulsford, later having decided that life under certain conditions of illness had no further potential for him, took matters into his own hands and drowned himself. This was long before discussions of death with dignity and beneficent euthanasia had become common, and before the right to suicide was affirmed in *Humanist Manifesto II* in 1973.

Pulsford had been a minister of the First Unitarian Church of Chicago. As students, Buschman and I heard him preach vigorous and brilliant sermons. He wrote to Bragg on May 28, 1933:

> The "Humanist Manifesto" interests me much. As you

perhaps know I am in fundamental agreement with the position it sets forth. I should however like to modify the third affirmation so as to avoid the traditional dualism between man and "nature" or, were I to use the old phraseology, between man and God. That would be done were the second affirmation to read somewhat as follows:—

"Humanism believes that man has emerged as one of the phases of a continuous cosmic process."

Were the Manifesto stripped of its negations and brought into key with the above by slight verbal alterations it would adequately express my own position.

The above comment (you invite expressions of opinion) is set forth in the last sentence of my little "Religion and the Modern Outlook," in relation to the aims of Humanism, thus:—

"A well reasoned faith that the possibilities of human life are integral with the unfolding process of the earth is the firm foundation on which, in all such movements, a justifiable confidence must ultimately rest." It is the dualism spoken of above which to me invalidates Bertrand Russell's "Free Man's Worship." . . .

If my suggestion seems to you worthwhile, you are of course free to discuss it with your co-adjutors, to the number of whom I like to feel that I too belong.

Pulsford's wisdom came too late to influence the editorial process, but in the perspective of years it is probable that he would have given wise guidance to the resolutions of the differences over the third and sixth theses.

Frank H. Hankins

Social scientist Frank H. Hankins was named a Humanist Pioneer by the American Humanist Association in 1960. His citation read that, "as author and teacher he set forth the tenets of evolutionary naturalism, identifying himself fully with the position of Roy Wood Sellars." The citation states that, because of his chapter on "Myth, Magic, Religion, and Science" in his *Studies in the Social Sciences*, the book became very controversial and led to one teacher losing his job because he used the book, another only kept her job on condition that she would drop it. Allegedly because of its radical naturalism, Macmillan would not publish a second edition.

On May 25, 1933, Hankins sent this letter from Smith College in Northampton, Massachusetts:

> I have received several letters regarding the Manifesto, indicating that there is a genuine interest in its content. The Bristol (Rhode Island) paper sent me a marked copy containing an editorial denouncing the signers in vigorous terms. The gist of the editorial was what ought to be done to the signers was to give them a good stiff slug in the jaw. Naturally one cannot enter into controversy with such people.
>
> I think there is no doubt that the 14th point to which you refer is more or less ambiguous. I am rather inclined to think that this ambiguity was a factor in securing signatures. This may not be pleasing to you, but I rather think it represents the situation. Personally, I would not wish to commit myself to a definite statement adopting anything like a Socialist creed. My sociological theory is that every society makes some sort of amalgam of individualism, state socialism, and communism. This amalgam, moreover, changes with every fundamental change in the material basis of culture. It is therefore unscientific as well as unwise to commit oneself to a *prioristic* or dogmatic statement of just what combination of these principles should be made at any time. Personally, I should hope that "a socialized and cooperative economic order" could be established without surrendering very important values in the principles of individual liberty, initiative and private property. If, however, it should be decided to attempt an enlargement of the 14th point, I should be glad to give the matter due consideration.

Charles Francis Potter

Charles Francis Potter, writing at length to Bragg on May 1, said:

Your letter and the three manifesto releases did not reach my office until today, as they were not mailed in Chicago until Saturday evening and there is no mail delivery on Sunday in New York, except special delivery. It is now too late to do anything with them, for if any one of the three services, AP, IP, and UP, is favored, the other two will cut the release dead unless it is big news. You could have given the release to the other news services at their Chicago offices at the same time as AP, and you would have secured nation-wide coverage.

I hope you sent advance copies to the columnists, such as Elsie Robinson, who does "Listen, World." She has the largest audience of any columnist, 15,000,000 readers daily, and is much interested in Humanism. She gave us a whole column when we started here, and another column when my book on Humanism came out.

If you wanted to tie up the story to *The New Humanist*, you could have done it beautifully by having it appear in your magazine's next issue, and releasing a newspaper story to break before the day of issue, saying,—"*The New Humanist* will publish tomorrow an exclusive article announcing. . . ." Of course, you had a little tie-up by including Wilson's name as editor of *The New Humanist*, but the AP story was cut in *The NY Herald-Tribune*, for instance, both in content and names, and Wilson's name was one of those left out. My issue of the *NY Times* carried no story whatever. If you had wired me, as I suggested, I could have seen the editor, whom I know personally, yesterday and would have impressed him with the significance of the thing and he would have got Dewey, Barnes, or Randall on the wire for a local supplementary statement. I just talked on the wire with Stanley Walker, city editor of the *Herald-Tribune*, trying to get him to run a follow-up story tomorrow, but he thought the half-column he ran today was adequate. *The Daily News* ran a little story. *The World-Telegram* had nothing, but that was becaue UP didn't have the release. . . .

Let me congratulate you and Wilson on the good work you put in on this manifesto. I know how hard it is to get liberals to agree on anything. The thing is historic, and its importance will gradually be recognized. I think the theists are more scared of us than they admit.

Bragg responded promptly on May 4:

You are aware of my lack of acquaintance with the methods of publicity. From this time I shall feel more adequate to the task of getting news before the American public. There were many slips and omissions incidental to the issuing of the Manifesto. There is little excuse for a great many of them. But the fact that my fiscal year was ending at the time work on the Manifesto became most trying explains part of the difficulty.

We had some good publicity here though the *Tribune* wrote it down as it would be expected. *The Herald-Examiner* gave a very decent presentation and a fairly complete one. The really interesting part of it will come later. I have indications that the *Christian Century* is going to blow things up pretty decidedly. Charles Lyttle phoned me this morning in something of a huff that he had not been drawn into the preparation of the statement. He told me of a meeting of the Christian Church History Society last night at which Garrison had said that the *Century* was going to do a job on it. Let it be so. Holmes was asked to sign and he replied in two letters portions of which will appear in *The New Humanist*. His mind is so firm that it is not easy to discuss these matters with him. He talks very vaguely about man leaping beyond himself. Now can't you imagine John (Haynes) Holmes leaping beyond himself? It sounds rather ridiculous when it is brought down to specific incidents.

You will be interested to know that this morning I received a splendid letter from my old teacher Walter Goodnow Everett commending us all for issuing the statement. He declares that after a life time of reflection of matters pertaining to religion he comes to the conclusion that we are "everlastingly right."

The correspondence continued on May 13, with Dr. Potter's remarks on John Haynes Holmes of special interest:

The May-June issue of *The New Humanist* is a fine piece of work. I hope there were plenty of extra copies printed, for there is sure to be a continuing demand for them. . . .

In reply to your letter of May 4, let me say that I wasn't

at all surprised that Holmes refused to sign the manifesto. He has reverted to theism since he was over and saw Gandhi, whose simple faith in God made a great impression on Holmes. The latter has a very theistic order of service. He is also very pessimistic about the future of liberal religion, but that is partly due to his physical condition and partly to his sad experience with his apartment-hotel proposition.

Nor was I surprised to hear that Morgan and Buschman wouldn't sign. The former wouldn't sign anything which anyone else wrote, and the latter has never been a real Humanist and never will be happy until he severs relations with the rest of us. As for Otto, I was much surprised. If the manifesto is an ineffectual gesture and a tactical error, what would he propose? Doing nothing at all for fear we should do something wrong?

There are plenty of men who are proud to be known as Humanists but who are unwilling to commit themselves to a cooperative program. The Unitarians have made the error of super-individualism, and I hope that Humanism will not stumble over the same stool.

I have read carefully the objections of these four men, all of whom I honor highly, but I think their points are weak.

The effect of the manifesto in New York has been distinctly beneficial, both outside our society and inside.

I am glad that Everett wrote you. If he is the Brown University Everett,[1] he called at one of our meetings on his way South last year and was very enthusiastic for Humanism.

If you have any extra copies of the Chicago papers' articles on the manifesto, please slip them in your next letter. I think I sent you a copy of the *N.Y. Herald-Tribune* story, which was the best here.

Shortly after this, Dr. Potter again wrote to Bragg:

Let me know how much stuff your clippings-bureau collects. I'm always interested to see which papers pick up a liberal religious release. We are having trouble all the time

---

1. W. G. Everett was the Brown University philosophy professor whom Potter met.

with the Roman Catholics' bringing all the possible pressure to bear to keep Humanism out of the news.

Humanism is getting quite a bit of good publicity through the Pearl Buck case because it is tied up with the laymen's Foreign Mission Inquiry Report, "Rethinking Missions," which has been assailed here as "pure Humanism" because it calls for education in place of evangelism in the future mission work.

P.S. LATER—

I just got in touch with the chief editor of United Press and tried to get him to take something of the manifesto on a rewrite or anything, but he is sore that the AP got a scoop on him, and he won't print a thing. There is great rivalry, you know, which is why extreme care has to be used not to let one have it an hour before the other.

Yes, I knew that Walker was once speaker of the Mass. House and candidate for the governorship. He is a good man. So is Auer. Are you going to collect and publish a list of additional names? If you got each of these 34 to work on it, you could easily get at least a hundred good names. If only 20 out of the 34 got 5 names each, it would make the hundred.

It would be a good move to have all the Humanist preachers take the manifesto for a sermon—or a series of sermon-subjects. I am preaching on it next Sunday.

We are going to keep our headquarters open all summer, and our preaching services five weeks longer than usual.

In his reply, Bragg wrote:

We have no money for clipping service. The money that has gone into the preparation of the manifesto thus far has come from the pockets of Wilson, Reese, and myself. We cannot do more. We shall have to depend on various ministers sending in clippings. Already I have had word from Kansas City, Quincy, Ill., about stories appearing in papers in those cities. It is disappointing that nothing got into the *Times*, is it not? I assume a great deal of responsibility for most of the omissions.

It is obvious that neither Bragg nor I had the public-relations expertise at that time which could have enabled us to make this event front-page news. Dr. Potter, had he had the materials in hand on the right date, probably would have been able to do it. In spite of our ignorance of the inner workings of the media, "A Humanist Manifesto" got through to a number of newspapers and, particularly, to the religious press.

CHAPTER 16

Six Years Later:
A Call to Revise the Manifesto

A s we've seen, soon after "A Humanist Manifesto" was published in 1933, there were those who, for various reasons, wanted a revision of the document, and the call continued in the ensuing years. Dr. Charles Francis Potter, who had reprinted the manifesto in his 1933 book, *Humanizing Religion*, brought the issue to an unavoidable point in 1939, when he mailed a letter to most of the original signers stating that there was a great need for reprinting the manifesto but that his focus was on a new or revised edition. On March 22, 1939, Dr. Potter wrote to Dr. Bernard Fantus of the College of Medicine at the University of Illinois at Chicago:

> You will remember that at the time the Manifesto was drawn up a number of those who signed it were not in full agreement with all its theses or with its phraseology. It was announced that it was a tentative form and would probably be changed.
>
> Nearly six years have elapsed and no changes have been made. Meanwhile the world has been rolling along and we have had more light on the thought of Humanism. I think that the time has come for a revision of the Manifesto, and I believe that the number of signatures could be greatly increased.
>
> I am writing this letter to ask you, as a signer of the Manifesto, if you think it should be revised, and, if so,

in what way. If a considerable number agree that it should be changed, a committee can get to work on it.

These paragraphs were apparently in the letter sent to the other signers. On that same day, Potter wrote to me in greater length:

We have had such a call for copies of the Humanist Manifesto that I have had it printed with an introduction taken from my book, "Humanizing Religion." It was available only in that book and in a back number of the New Humanist. I am enclosing a copy herewith as a sample.

Nearly six years have elapsed and no changes have been made. Meanwhile the world has been rolling along and we have had more light on the thought of Humanism. I think that the time has come for a revision of the Manifesto, and I believe that the number of signatures could be greatly increased. For instance, I think that the eighth thesis might well be rephrased to include the point that man is an end in himself and not a means to the glory of God or the glory of the totalitarian state. What do you think about it?

Recently I have come into contact with a number of Humanists outside the Unitarian fold, many of them prominent in executive positions in social reform work. I have sat in conference with them, one time with over a hundred, and there are some significant developments impending. They are working on a statement of principles much resembling the Manifesto, but arrived at independently of it.

A month ago I was in Washington and conferred with several leading men there. There seems to be a feeling on the part of many of the real leaders of America that the current proposition to unite Catholics, Jews and Protestants in a three-faith movement for the strengthening of democracy will not adequately solve the problem facing our country, largely because of the difficulty of reconciling supernaturalistic theism with the modern scientific point-of-view. Humanism seems to be looked upon with increasing favor as a possible basic philosophy, at least for those Americans who have no connection with any existing religious organization.

I am sending this letter to several who signed the Manifesto and would appreciate hearing from you at your convenience. If there is a general agreement that the Manifesto should be revised, we can then plan to go ahead and do it.

Dr. Potter's letters brought a quick reaction from the signatories, including the four of us who comprised the editorial committee of "A Humanist Manifesto." On March 28, 1939, Bragg wrote to me from Minneapolis, where he was minister of the First Unitarian Society (succeeding John H. Dietrich):

> Did you have a letter from Potter about revising the Humanist Manifesto? I rather suspect that the same letters went to all signers of the original document. We will have to answer the letter in the not too distant future and ought to be pointing in the same direction. . . . Write me promptly about your inclination in this matter.

Bragg reflected the general opinion of the Chicago group that, if a revision were to be attempted, it should be by the Humanist Press Association, which held the copyright. The feeling was that, because of his flare for publicity, humanism might become too exclusively identified with Potter. Moreover, at least one HPA officer felt that Potter's actions to initiate revision were presumptuous. I, too, was somewhat of a promoter and admired Dr. Potter's publicity skills. We had worked together in the past to try to keep *The New Humanist* afloat.[1] Caught in the middle, I tried to mediate.

Letters about the revision idea kept coming to Dr. Fantus, who at the time was bedfast. Dr. Fantus wrote to me on March 29, 1939, referring to Potter's "circular letter" of March 28:

> For the last few days I have amused myself by writing enclosed modification of "The Manifesto" which I did

---

1. By this time, *The New Humanist* had ceased publication due to lack of funding. Additionally, in 1936 a fire destroyed the building of the Third Unitarian Church, and it was my responsibility to raise the funds to rebuild the church, a task that took up a great deal of my time and energy. However, in 1938, by popular demand, and under the auspices of the Humanist Press Association, I started a newsletter called *The Humanist Bulletin*, which filled the gap between the cessation of *The New Humanist* and the commencement in 1941 of *The Humanist*.

without any other idea than attempting to express suggestions that, in my opinion, "The Manifesto" as we have it at present is somewhat too scholastic to serve the purpose of a document that might set the world aflame. Believe you will agree with me that nothing but a religious flame can save the world from a holocaust that may mean the sacrifice of most of our human civilization as we know it today.

Dr. Fantus penciled a first draft on the back of Dr. Potter's March 22 letter. This deathbed revision, entitled "A Humanist's Affirmation," was printed and widely circulated. Dr. Fantus felt that the ideas he included were needed in the world; he sought to affirm that which could guide men and women of widely differing circumstances. As I later described Fantus at his funeral, I said: "In his quiet, efficient way, he combined a command of scientific method, creative imagination, practical skill, and humanitarian idealism as have few men in our time." Three days after his memorial service, the new clinics of the Cook County Hospital in Illinois were formally dedicated as the Bernard Fantus Clinics.

Raymond Bragg wrote to me again in April 1939, stating that he could not get to Chicago for a meeting of the HPA executive committee which I had proposed. He said:

I am writing to Potter saying that some of the Chicago men are meeting next week, that nothing can be done until we hear from the Chicago group. Certainly we can take the position that things center in the H.P.A. and that independent action is inadequate.

The Reverend John Hershey, a personal friend and correspondent of mine (who held special concern for Latin and South American humanists), aggravated the situation by circulating extracts from a personal letter he had received from me. One recipient was Joseph Walker, the prominent Boston attorney who had signed the manifesto. Hershey's letter contained quotes from me, without my knowledge or consent. This letter was also sent to Professor J. A. C. F. Auer and Albert Dieffenbach, then editor of the *Christian Register.* The letter read:

> I send you herewith extracts from a letter that has come
> to me from Ed Wilson. You will note that he suggests (1)
> non-cooperation with Mr. Potter and (2) a method for
> revision of the Manifesto through committees.
>
> Ed writes me that he would very much like to have
> the opinion of the Boston signers of the Manifesto regard-
> ing these two matters. Will you kindly advise him what
> you think should be done? . . .

I then wrote to my friend Hershey:

> I doubt that it was wise of you to copy my personal letter
> to you and send extracts on to Walker or anyone else, John.
> I was quite frank with you and I am hopeful that you know
> that Mr. Walker is not a close friend and admirer of Pot-
> ter's. It would jamb things up. Please don't quote from my
> letters to you in writing to anyone as I'm accustomed to
> being franker with you than I might be on certain diplo-
> matic matters in print.

John Hershey's intentions were good, but I urged him
to tell Walker that the letter had been personal, from me to
Hershey. I also said that I would have Hershey's status as
representative of HPA in Boston confirmed by the executive
committee.

My letter to Hershey had expressed concern about procedure and was not meant to derogate Dr. Potter. Behind the
attitudes apprehensive of unilateral action by Potter was the
suspicion (perhaps tinged with envy) of both the liberal ministers and academic colleagues of anyone who could draw
a crowd or make the headlines as did Charles Francis Potter.

The files contain an unsigned and undated carbon of a
letter written by either Bragg or me—probably a draft of one
mailed to the signers of the 1933 document. It reads:

> Charles Potter of N.Y. has taken unto himself the task of
> revising the Humanist Manifesto. I gave him permission
> to reprint the Manifesto in *his book*, but he did not ask
> or receive permission to reprint it, as he has, under the

the name of his Society. He has written all signers of the Humanist Manifesto.

I am writing men in various parts of the country asking them to get in touch with nearby manifesto signers asking them to send any opinions or suggested revisions of the Manifesto to the H.P.A. and *not* to cooperate with Potter. He has not asked permission or cooperation from our organization although he did write me as if he were proposing the revision but apparently at the same time he wrote these other men.

. . . I suggest a committee, perhaps including Potter, to go on with the revision. Perhaps studies of the Manifesto in three or four cities culminating in a central committee correlating the material. What do you think?

Albert C. Dieffenbach expressed his opinion in a letter he wrote on April 10, 1939, in Cambridge, Massachusetts, in which he stated—a judgment that ultimately prevailed—that "A Humanist Manifesto" was a dated document to be interpreted in terms of the situation at the time of its publication. As a journalist as well as a liberal minister, he appreciated (as did I) Dr. Potter's publicity skills; however, he disagreed with him on a revision. His letter read:

I have already written Charles Potter I'm against revision. This was a manifesto, and *is*, a thing not to be changed any more than the Declaration of Independence, the 39 Articles, or such, may be changed. There may be addenda or the equivalent of amendments, but the Manifesto is there, once and for all. I have so told Auer, with whom I labored on the original at the insistence of Ray Bragg with great pains. Auer's contribution was very great. I believe he and I agree on this, but by all means keep peace and fellowship with Potter who is a potent ally and propagator of Humanism.

On April 10, 1939, I wrote to Charles Potter:

I have been discussing your suggestion of the Humanist Manifesto. It is not a new idea as it has come up now and again. The feeling was that we needed a more explicit statement, or program.

Curtis Reese, Eustace Haydon and Ray Bragg all agree that the matter should be handled through the Humanist Press Association. A meeting of the Executive Committee will be held this week to confirm the appointment of a committee on revision which will include the original committee plus several others.

The committee which drafted the Manifesto was composed of Roy Wood Sellars, A. E. Haydon, R. B. Bragg, Curtis Reese, and myself. We would like to have you serve on the new committee. Probably J. A. C. F. Auer and E. A. Burtt will also be asked to serve.

There is one point which needs to be thrashed out and that is whether we should let the old Manifesto stand for what it was—the statement of a developing position at a particular time and proceed to a new statement striking at the present world crisis and command the cooperation of men like Benes, Thomas Mann, Einstein, et cetera. What do you think?

I feel, personally, that this is the best way to handle revision. There are various viewpoints which need to be represented by a committee representative of all and not too closely to any one of them.

By this time, Dr. Potter, who regularly addressed meetings of the First Humanist Society of New York at Steinway Hall, had gathered a notable list of sponsors. As members of his advisory board, his letterhead lists over thirty well-known people, including John Dewey, Will Durant, Helen Keller, James H. Leuba, Herbert Bayard Swope, and Oswald Garrison Villard. Later the name of Albert Einstein would be added. Dr. Potter realized the worldwide potential of humanism and the value of prestigious names. His letter to me, dated April 12, 1939, shows his global vision of humanism as well as his willingness to cooperate with others:

I have your letter of the 10th and agree that the matter of the proposed revision of the 1933 Manifesto or the issuing of a new one should be handled through the H.P.A. And I accept your invitation to serve on the committee. Auer and Burtt would make good members.

As for the choice between revising the 1933 Manifesto

or issuing a new one, I incline toward the latter course. Several of the 16 men who have answered my letter urge letting the old statement stand as a dated document, although they do not now agree with all its theses as they are phrased. Most of them, however, indicated some revision they would make if revision were decided upon.

Not only Benes, Mann, and Einstein, but also many other leaders would sign a new manifesto. I am in touch with many non-Unitarian humanists, especially among the social scientists. There is a surprising interest in religious humanism in Washington, D.C. I had a talk about humanism with Sec'y Hull in February, an appointment arranged by F.D.R. himself after he read my sermon in the N.Y. Times.

Dr. Borchard of Yale, expert on International law often consulted by Hull and Roosevelt, who went to Lima and back with Hull, is a member of our society here, and has been talking humanism to them. Several other administration men are humanists.

I think we have a splendid chance to get some top-notch scientists to sign a manifesto, for I have talked with a number of them and they are distinctly on our side. I have recently been invited to address the next annual convention of the [American Academy for the Advancement of Science] on Humanism and Science. That grew out of a three-day conference with 100 social scientists in Washington a year ago. This group has just adopted the term "Scientific Humanism" to describe their belief.

Dr. Har Dayal of India and London, a splendid scholar who could lecture fluently in eight languages, spoke for me here on "Why I Am a Humanist," and joined our society, but, alas, he just died of a heart attack.

Auer was down last week and we had a long session, discussing the manifesto.

Burtt is speaking for me next Sunday and I will talk with him about it. Aronson speaks for me the 30th, and I'm sure he would sign. We ought to get at least a hundred good names.

As the representative of the HPA executive committee, I then sent a questionnaire to a select number of humanists:

The Executive Committee of the Humanist Press Association feels that the question of revision or of making a new declaration should be handled by a representative committee of the HPA. They are inclined to let the first Manifesto stand as a dated document and issue a new statement along new lines. Will you please fill in and return the enclosed blank as a preliminary step.

A Project for a Humanist Declaration of Faith in Man

Committee: C. W. Reese, Chairman; E. H. Wilson, Secretary; J. A. C. F. Auer; E. A. Burtt; R. B. Bragg; A. E. Haydon; R. W. Sellars; M. C. Otto; C. F. Potter

1. Do you personally prefer (1) a revision of the original Manifesto (1933) or (2) a new declaration?
2. Make any suggestions or comments on this sheet or in accompanying letter as to methods, objectives of developing the new affirmation.
3. Please list here topics that you believe need to be covered or try your hand at a first draft of such a statement.
4. What title would you suggest for the new declaration? (As for instance "Humanist Declaration of Faith and Action".)
5. List here or on additional sheet names and addresses of leaders, in addition to signers of the original Manifesto, who should be asked to sign the new one.

In going through the files, I found records of only three responses to my letter (although it's possible there might have been more in subsequent correspondence). These three commentators—R. W. Sellars, M. C. Otto, and E. A. Burtt (coincidentally all philosophers and members of the revision committee)—all preferred a new statement rather than a revision of the 1933 manifesto. Each of them responded to all the questions, but the following quotes are their answers to the second point. Professor Burtt wrote:

> You have probably considered the question of how much this Manifesto is to take in—how much of the world. That constitutes a problem. If you take in too much territory, the statement will tend to be vague; if too little territory, it will not be a representative statement. And I hope any Manifesto sent out will be characteristic of the humility

which its situation calls for.

Professor Sellars wrote that the declaration "must not be too journalistic but stress principles and indicate their implications." Professor Otto replied: "Let us try to rally with us all who have faith in the possibility of a finer life for men and women through intelligent cooperation."

Ultimately, a committee meeting proved impossible, as members were just too widespread and there was no funding for travel expenses. Clearly this was frustrating to Dr. Potter, who wrote me a number of times alternately expressing his eagerness to see a new document and his frustration with the HPA committee that just "fizzled out."

CHAPTER 17

Twenty Years Later:
Symposium—Parts I and II

While the first manifesto was never revised, debate over
the need for revision or for a new document continued.
So much so, that twenty years later, a symposium was published containing the views of the twenty-seven surviving
signers (John Dewey, Bernard Fantus, William Floyd, Maynard Shipley, W. Frank Swift, Joseph Walker, and Frank S. C.
Wicks had all died) as well as a selection of other humanists.
However, before discussing that symposium, let us get an over-
view of the interim twenty years.

The Humanist *Moves East*

In August 1941, I moved from Chicago to the Unitarian pulpit
at Schenectady, New York, for a five-year war-time ministry.
With the encouragement of Corliss Lamont and Max Otto,
I resumed publication of *The New Humanist*, now as editor
and under the altered title, *The Humanist*. The word *new* was
deleted from the title to help disassociate the movement from
the literary humanism of Irving Babbitt and Paul Elmer More.

At the same time in 1941, following the organizational
insights of Curtis Reese, the name of the magazine's sponsor
was changed from the Humanist Press Association to the
American Humanist Association. We had become more than
just a publishing organization; we were now a fellowship of

like-minded supporters of a cause generating commitment. Over the next decade, the membership and magazine circulation grew. By 1952, *The Humanist* had correspondents in Denmark, England, France, India, Israel, Italy, Japan, Latin America, West Germany, Sweden, and Uruguay. In addition to serving as editor, I was devoting most of my time serving as executive director of the AHA from its offices in Yellow Springs, Ohio.

A Point of Controversy

Because various philosophic points of view emerge religiously and ethically as humanism, there came a time in the 1940s when there was a rather vigorous complaint that the editorial policy of *The Humanist* was too pragmatic in its orientation. (This was the position of philosopher Arthur Murphy who chose to drop out.) Roy Wood Sellars was a critical realist and therefore, in epistemology, anti-Dewey. Eventually there was also a rather sharp conflict between the logical positivists, as represented by Charles Morris, John Dewey, and Arthur Bentley, and conflict between Bertrand Russell and John Dewey.

The International Humanist and Ethical Union

Also in 1952, an important, historic event took place: with the founding of the International Humanist and Ethical Union, humanism became an organized world movement. The IHEU filed incorporation papers in New York and established its international headquarters in Utrecht, the Netherlands. It stated in its "Declaration of the Founding Congress, Amsterdam, 1952":

> The primary task of humanism to-day is to make men aware in the simplest terms of what it can mean to them and what it commits them to. By utilizing in this context, and for purposes of peace, the new power which science has given

us, humanists have confidence that the present crisis can be surmounted. Liberated from fear the energies of man will be available for a self-realization to which it is impossible to foresee the limit.

Ethical humanism is thus a faith that answers the challenge of our times. We call upon men who share this conviction to associate themselves with us.

The Symposium: Part I

In the March/April 1953 issue of *The Humanist* (13:2:63–71), a symposium was published which included the original manifesto; "An Historical Note" by Raymond Bragg; an article by Roy Wood Sellars entitled "Naturalistic Humanism: A Framework for Belief and Values"; as well as the responses of the surviving signatories (and preselected others) to the questions: "How has the manifesto stood the test of time?" and "If a new statement were to be prepared today, what changes should be made?"

Roy Wood Sellars. Having drafted the original manifesto, the editors at *The Humanist* were pleased that Sellars agreed to write an article for the symposium, which read in part:

> Much has happened since the formulation and the publication of the *Humanist Manifesto*. Under able and vigorous leadership in this and other countries, Humanism has become an international stream of thought and commitment aiming at a basic revision of the human outlook and a revaluation of values. I still think the adjective, naturalistic, best symbolizes the perspective of religious Humanism since it calls attention to its rejection of supernaturalism. Modern naturalism is, inevitably, evolutionary in its premises. . . . As I see it, it is all a matter of accent. The essential thing is to have a common framework.
>
> Is Humanism a religion, perhaps, the next great religion? Yes, it must be so characterized, for the word, religion, has become a symbol for answers to that *basic interrogation* of human life, the human situation, and the nature of things—which every human being, in some degree

and in some fashion, makes. What can I expect from life? What kind of universe is it? Is there, as some say, a friendly Providence in control of it? And, if not, what then? The universe of discourse of religion consists of such questions, and the answers relevant to them. Christian theism and Vedantic mysticism are but historic frameworks in relation to which answers have in the past been given to these poignant and persistent queries. But there is nothing sacrosanct and self-certifying about these frameworks. What Humanism represents is the awareness of another framework, more consonant with wider and deeper knowledge about man and his world. The Humanist movement is engaged in formulating answers, with what wisdom it can achieve, to these basic questions.

. . . The Humanist outlook is based on the empirical fact of evolutionary levels in nature. Man has abilities which are unique and which rest on his capacity for symbolism because it is magnified by cultural inheritance. Each generation begins where the prior generation left. The reductionist is simply one who ignores what biological and social evolution have wrought, and has eyes for inorganic themes. The mechanical materialist is of the same vintage. Modern quantum mechanics is primarily mathematical and is not tied in with fixed, mechanical models and pictures. The patterned subtlety of nature, as exhibited in biochemistry, for instance, is not denied but given an *historical dimension*, one step making possible another step. . . .

In conclusion, I want to contrast the perspective of humanism with that of traditional rationalism. . . . The older rationalism was on the defensive. And so it expressed itself too often in negative terms; *not* this; *not* that; not God; not revelation; not personal immortality. What Humanism signified was a shift from negation to construction. There came a time when naturalism no longer felt on the defensive. Rather, supernaturalism began, in its eyes, to grow dim and fade out despite all the blustering and rationalizations of its advocates.

Now this was a change in dominance, long prepared in both philosophy and science, and beginning to manifest itself in everyday life. To use a homely expression, the shoe was on the other foot. Instead of feeling that he had to disprove the existence of a God, special revelation, and

the general *mystique* of a supernatural realm, the naturalist simply began with good reason to feel that the job of
proving these pivotal assumptions rested with the super-
naturalist. And he knew that both theologians and philosophers in the past had never been able to develop satisfactory
proofs. In short, the strategic situation had changed.

As I conceived it, then, the *Humanist Manifesto* expressed this change of dominance as a sort of declaration
of independence. And I imagine that Wilson and the others
who supplied the comments and suggestions which went
into its making had something similar in mind. Naturalism
was maturing into a humanistic phase. The old supernaturalistic framework no longer possessed its former
intrinsic prestige. There were now *two* competing frames
of reference for both belief and values. The time had come
for a reassessment all along the line. If possible, a friendly
debate was indicated. Let the premises or theses be stated
and the arguments, pro and con, be entered. To the best
of our knowledge, what kind of a universe are we in? What
can man expect? Is man now his own worst enemy? What
are the complexities of human nature? In what fashion are
these tied in with cultural arrangements? What can be done
about it?

I have recently read over the fifteen theses. On the
whole, I think they sketch the essentials of a framework
which is both naturalistic and humanistic. There is, of
course, nothing sacrosanct about any of the formulations.
New conditions will bring new emphases. . . .

The Signers Reappraise. In their introduction to the symposium, *The Humanist*'s editors included a statement which is
really a fine definition of humanism:

> This present reappraisal is a continuation of the constant
> effort to keep Humanism a dynamic movement. Humanists
> do not look back to a faith delivered once and for all time
> at a particular moment or during a particular period in his-
> tory. They rather look forward to a constantly growing syn-
> thesis produced by the interaction of many minds relating
> the increasing discoveries of science to human fulfillment.

From his "Historical Note" of introduction, Ray Bragg wrote:

. . . The Manifesto had a wide press coverage. *Time, The Literary Digest, The Christian Century,* the Associated Press, religious journals representing a variety of denominations sent it into every corner of this country. The late Clarence Skinner thought it might some day rank with Luther's more extensive theses. Catholic journals presented it as the logical outcome of the centuries of Protestant thought.

The immediate aims were achieved: to stir up discussion, to prompt debate. The editorial note accompanying the publication was explicit on that score. And, for the greater part, that spirit was carried in the reporting of the document.

To revise the Manifesto, in my estimation, would be misfortunate. If Humanists in 1953 or 1954 want to restate the position, let it be done in today's terms. Twenty years ago the editors were careful in their designation. The document of 1933 was called *A* Humanist Manifesto. Each living signer has pondered many meanings since that time. Nonetheless, in 1933 he stood by what he signed, whatever qualifications he may have made in his own mind or for the informal record.

A new formulation may be in order. May the vigorous undertake it!

There followed the comments of the signatories in the exact order of their appearance in the symposium:

J. A. C. Fagginger Auer (Cambridge, Massachusetts):

I have read the Manifesto over and I do not think I should want to change anything at the present moment. Even the fourteenth point does not disturb me very much. I believe we still want a socialized and co-operative economic order to the end that equitable distribution of the means of life be possible. I see nothing revolutionary in it and a good deal that is commendable.

E. Burdette Backus (Indianapolis, Indiana):

On the whole, I should be willing to sign the Manifesto again as it now stands. Some of the points I might want to modify to a slight extent. For instance, in the first one

I should like to include the statement that I regard the universe as itself creative. The suggestive material in Hoyle, *The Nature of the Universe*, indicating that the creative process is going on all the while is a case in point. Similarly, under point eleven I should like to be more specific about using the social sciences, particularly psychology, as instruments for securing Humanist objectives.

As to point fourteen, I am convinced that it is descriptive of an historic trend which has by no means played itself out. Norman Thomas is doubtless right in his new pamphlet, "Democratic Socialism, A New Appraisal," in his statement that developments of recent years compel a revision in our thinking on certain traditional socialist doctrines. None the less it still seems to me clear that we shall have to achieve a much greater degree of socialization if we are to promote the Humanist purpose of fulfilling personal lives.

Even as it stands the Manifesto is still a significant document and I am proud to have been one of the original signers.

Harry Elmer Barnes (Cooperstown, New York):

A careful reading of the Humanist Manifesto convinces me that it has stood up remarkably well considering the fact that the last twenty years have been the most dynamic and world-shaking, for evil as well as good, but more for evil than good, in the history of mankind. Some additions might be desirable but it would not be necessary to retreat from any main position taken.

I would criticize the seventh proposition, not in the light of any changes since 1933, but because of what I believed to be a serious defect when stated in 1933. Humanists should be able to define religion more precisely or not try to define it at all. The definition in the seventh point is too loose and inclusive to mean anything at all. The words "art," "education," "philosophy," "ethics," etc. could be substituted for the term religion and the statement would read just as soundly as it does now. Religion may be interested in all the fields and activities mentioned, but it does not "consist of" them. Or it may represent a special approach to, or evaluation of, these fields and human interests. But, as it stands, the definition is vague and worthless and could be used to base a charge that the Humanists do not actually know what religion is.

In point fourteen, I would leave out the word "socialized" and say "a free and co-operative" economy. It is symptomatic of the changed temper of the times that what would have been regarded as a mildly conservative economic statement in 1933 might well lead to the charge in 1953 that Humanists are "security risks."

It might be well to add something which would indicate the transformations that have taken place in the main challengers to Humanism between 1933 and 1953. In the religious field in 1933 fundamentalism, Catholic and Protestant, was the main menace or challenge to Humanism. Today, it is more Niebuhrism, neo-orthodoxy, intellectual obfuscation, and the like. Humanism has successfully battled against antiscientific views of life which antedated modern science and Biblical criticism, but it has not made any systematic attack on the intellectualistic obscurantism led by Niebuhr and others which does not stem from fundamentalism, though it may have less logic to sustain itself and be less entitled to respect on the ground that its expositors should know better.

Far more menacing to Humanism and to the "good life" Humanism seeks to promote than fundamentalism, Niebuhrism, and related trends—or all combined—are the rise of globaloney and world-meddling, the conquest of internationalism by militarism, and the growing acceptance of a world system of "perpetual war for perpetual peace."

L. M. Birkhead (New York, New York):

The Manifesto seems to me to represent the thinking of enlightened religious liberals today as it did twenty years ago. I would leave out nothing.

In paragraph three the word "establish" should be changed to "develop." Humanists do not seek to establish a religion, but to develop their Humanist religion. And couldn't some word be added to point fourteen to indicate a less dogmatic economic point of view? There seems to me to be a paradox in the repudiation of capitalism in the early part of the paragraph and an expression of Humanist faith in "a free and universal society" at the end of the paragraph.

Edwin Arthur Burtt (Ithaca, New York):

The word "Humanism" still comes closer than any other to representing my general philosophic position. But I've gone a long way since 1933. And to square my present thinking with the details of the Manifesto would require that I complete, right now, what I hope to work out in a book some ten years in the future. Many issues of basic importance are involved.

Ernest Caldecott (Los Angeles, California):

I think the Manifesto is still very sound, but somewhat "stuffy." I would leave out nothing, but would change wordings here and there to make the document more semantically correct.

I would add between paragraphs fifteen and sixteen the following new paragraph: "Due to man's understanding of his own nature, and, therefore, of his fellows, it is imperative (that we explain) our faith in man. Wars constitute an individual aberration which traditional religions have not cured. A re-evaluation of the nature of man, to be applied in terms of his surroundings, will give hope and determination that we shall so arrange our thinking, ethics, and actions that war shall be no more."

A. J. Carlson (Chicago, Illinois):

I would change paragraph fourteen in the direction of paragraph two of the explanatory statement of July 24, 1952 [which read: "Point fourteen, especially, has been the object of criticism from various angles. It reflects the outlook of depression times. Since the Humanist Manifesto ought not to enter as far into controversial realms as did point fourteen nor to take an official position as a movement with regard to any particular economic system."].

I think the *social responsibility* of the individual might be pointed out more clearly.

Frank H. Hankins (Northampton, Massachusetts):

On the whole the Humanist Manifesto is still an acceptable statement. Nevertheless, it might still be rewritten in its entirety. Since Humanists do not pretend to dogmatic finality, there should be no loss of prestige in alterations.

If I were doing a complete rewriting, I would alter every statement. At the same time, since any statement requires consensus among the signers, I would not insist on rewriting any theses except the third, the seventh, and the fourteenth.

[Since the rest of Mr. Hankins's letter is too long to quote in its entirety, only his suggested revision of points three, seven, and fourteen are given below.]

Third—Humanists therefore hold that the traditional belief in the dualism of mind and body was one of the basic errors of human thought from earliest times. Humanists hold the organic view that mind is the functioning of living bodies. While this view denies the possibility of future life, it sanctifies efforts to free this life of poverty, crime, vice, and every human meanness.

Seventh—Sociological and historical researchers have shown that the essential core of religion is devotion to those social values which bind men together in cooperative effort for group preservation and mutual welfare; and that these values are discovered through human experiences. Among those discovered in recent times are devotion to truth as exemplified in the scientific mentality, the dignity of individual man, and the ideals of democracy. Humanism thus becomes the next logical step in religious evolution; it is the heir and creative fulfillment of the Renaissance, the Reformation, and the democratic revolutions.

Fourteenth—Since the goal of Humanism is the highest possible development of the personality of each consistent with the welfare of all, and since this is possible only in a society cherishing ideals of human liberty, equality, and fraternity, a society in which people voluntarily and intelligently co-operate for the common good, Humanism favors such changes in the social order as promise [of] a more equitable distribution of the material bases of a good life.

A. Eustace Haydon (Chicago, Illinois):

The introductory statement has stood up remarkably well. The description of religion is abreast of the findings of the most advanced scientific research in the field today. I would like to add only that beneath the threefold complex of world view, technique, and ideal which serve as the embodiment of a religion there are the driving desires which determine the values of the ideal, physical, personal, and social desires.

In the fifth statement I would leave out "cosmic" since it is clear that while there is no personal or supernatural guarantee, man as a part of nature does get support for his values in the balance of the natural order, in the age-old habits of biology, and in the sense of oneness with the planetary process.

In the sixth, I would express sympathetic understanding for these old forms of thinking which we must nevertheless now surrender.

For fourteen I would substitute a statement calling upon all phases of civilization and culture to serve the common-weal as their only right to exist—a new synthesis of culture around a human, social ideal. Around this it would be possible to make a full statement of the social program and the method of progress toward the ideal. In this it could be made very clear that any religion vital today must be secular.

Llewellyn Jones (Cambridge, Massachusetts):

I see in general nothing wrong with the Manifesto, and while certain small changes might be suggested, they would be debatable. And, after all, is it not wiser to leave it as it was: by now it is a part of history, a "source." We all realize that it is "of 1933."

If I were preparing a new statement today I might either leave out section fourteen or change it to read that any society, whether profit-motivated or not, must exist to serve all individuals; that is, make some protest against the idea that "natural law" in the old sense, or any independent law of economics—such as the laws of the Manchester school—must be given full rein.

In the present state of ethical and philosophical thinking I do not think you could add anything that would meet with the approval of surviving original signers or new signers if you contemplate having younger people sign a revised Manifesto.

Have you thought that changing or adding to the Humanist Manifesto involves one very ticklish point? How will you get the consent to any changes of the seven deceased signers? By hypothesis we are denied the use of the Ouija board. We cannot have two Manifestoes, the historic one with their signatures on it and a new one with new signatures on it. After all, the importance of the Manifesto was to state a broad position: to rally to our banner Humanists who had learned their Humanism from such diverse sources as the old rationalist movements, agnosticism, atheism of the Lewis type, and then the naturalistic philosophies of Santayana, Dewey, Woodbridge, Sellars, Russell, the logical positivists, and so on. Any attempt to be too exact or even too contemporary in the phrasing of the Manifesto will simply result in a sort of argumentative free-for-all.

Robert Morss Lovett (Chicago, Illinois):

I think the Manifesto is fine. I would change nothing.

Harold P. Marley (Chicago, Illinois):

The Manifesto is too long—too wordy. There is not enough coming to grips with reality in view of Spain, World War II, release of atomic energy, and release of peoples from colonial imperialism.

If I were to prepare such a statement today I would leave out nothing of the essence, but would sharply condense.

[A section of Mr. Marley's letter dealing with particular methods of reorganization of the Manifesto is here omitted for lack of space. The letter concludes with a suggested rewording for point fourteen.]

Fourteen—The radical changes in profit-motivated society, held to be necessary twenty years ago, have steadily been taking place. Today, we witness an unprecedented rise of people's movements, particularly in colonial and exploited areas of the globe. The vitality of such movements was demonstrated during World War II against a Fascist onslaught which was stopped but not destroyed.

The evil forces of fascism, wherever they may be, would again join together to risk a world holocaust, and the bloody civil strife which would inevitably break out in country after country, continent by continent. The unspeakable terrors of civil strife in an atom-bomb age can well be guessed.

Humanists face these awful consequences (already manifest to a degree) knowing that not only Humanism, but civilization itself, is at stake. We believe that conciliation is the answer to impending world conflict, and that economic justice to all peoples is the only solution for achieving lasting peace and harmony.

Lester Mondale (Philadelphia, Pennsylvania):

I am still very much in sympathy with the general tenor of the statement; in particular, the stress on centering religion on man rather than on worship of a transcendent divinity, the emphasis on the natural (which is not to say *naturalism*) as against the supernatural, on this life rather than on life in any other sphere or time.

[A section of Mr. Mondale's letter dealing with specific minor changes suggested in wording and emphasis is omitted here for lack of space.]

My first addition would be to substitute for point fourteen a statement showing recognition of the fact that the threat to the democratic and free world today is religion of a totalitarian kind (including communism), and that what is inescapable for the free nations is a humanistic outlook, rather than a mere anti-communism, behind which they can unite and rally to the offensive.

I should like to see incorporated in any future statement this fact: that the fruitage of the ethical, or shall we say humanistic, life is a lively and sustaining sense of cosmic at-homeness.

Again, I believe that no religious movement, or philosophical for that matter, can regard itself as contemporary without an explicit statement that recognizes the tragic character not only of man's perennial inability to grasp truth entire or practice justice without at the same time being in some degree unjust, but also of certain ineradicable contradictions in the nature of man, in all human association, and in the best of the virtues themselves. Hence, the kind of "personality realization" (point eight) I hope any future statement will feature is that of the hero of Greek tragedy, maimed and ruined albeit, by evils from which the gods themselves are not exempt, but at the same time transcending evils with the nobility of an Oedipus, or with the contagious morale (in contrast with the probably more factual wail of defeat of "My God, My God") of the Greek Gospel: "Forgive them, for they know not what they do."

Charles Francis Potter (New York, New York):

The Manifesto today looks antique and sententious. It is verbose and dogmatic: even shrill at times. It is dated and it squeaks. My! Didn't we think we were wonderful crusaders!

If I were to prepare such a statement today, I would omit "or cosmic" in the fifth thesis. Omit sixth thesis entirely. It is a gratuitous slap, and there are, for instance, "New Thought" preachers more "humanistic" than some Unitarian Humanists. In the eighth thesis omit "in the here and now" which is an unnecessary limitation of personality.

Condense the three-paragraph preamble to one which should be less vague and preachy. A little humility and modesty of statement wouldn't hurt our cause. In the third sentence of first paragraph of the preamble, include "psychology." Combine the first four theses into one. Note how the fourth duplicates the second. Rewrite the seventh thesis and include the twelfth in it by simply adding the adjectives "creative" and "joyful." *Rewrite fourteenth thesis in the light of recent history.*

Add more fervor, hope, and enthusiasm.

J. H. Randall, Jr. (New York, New York):

I originally signed the Manifesto in a spirit of general agreement, without quibbling over details. My own philosophical views I have long preferred to call naturalistic rather than humanistic, and while for the purposes of stating a religious position the differences are minor, they are there. Thus in Point Five, while there certainly has been discovered no "cosmic guarantee of human values" I have always wished that there were some emphasis on the fact that such values are and must be rooted in the natural conditions of human life. Religion has always seemed to me truncated when focused too narrowly upon man alone, without a sense of the encompassing presence of the nature that has generated man and his concerns.

On two points on which the Manifesto failed to satisfy me I have come to feel more strongly. First, there is lacking any expression of a tragic sense of life. "Joy in living" (point 12) is not the only attitude religion must foster. There is also such a thing as humility. The inevitabilities of frustration and the evil that men necessarily do must be seen in proper perspective, but they must be seen. There is no reason why supernaturalism should be allowed a monopoly on the religious expression of this tragic sense. Humanism can do it more effectively because more sanely. Thus, in the last paragraph, "man has within himself the power for the achievement of the world of his dreams," has always sounded insensitive and brash. Man has the power to work toward it, and there is no other power. But . . .

Secondly, there is insufficient recognition of the need of imagination in religion, and of the role of religious symbols. The traditional Christian symbols are no longer adequate—though they seem much more relevant to present-day experience than to that of a generation ago. But no religion that tries to get along without any imaginative embodiment of its basic attitudes and values is likely to attract many. Humanism should face seriously the very difficult problem of creating more adequate imaginative symbols. It should at least recognize the need even if it cannot yet satisfy it.

Both these points demand much further elaboration, especially the second, to which I have given a great deal of attention and thought. But I think the problems suggested will be sufficiently indicated to any one who has lived through the last twenty years with some sensitive attention to the direction of religious feeling and thought.

Curtis W. Reese (Chicago, Illinois):

The Manifesto seems to me today as valid as it was in 1933. I would change nothing and add only a more extensive statement of the implications of the scientific method and spirit—clearly implied in point five.

The controversy about point fourteen appears to me to be much ado about nothing. By no stretch of the imagination can point fourteen be made to support Soviet Communism. We must not allow our anticommunistic attitude to swing us out of accord with the world-wide trend toward a more socialized economy. The sentence beginning "The goal of humanism . . ." was written by me, and was designed to put point fourteen in definite opposition to totalitarianisms of all kinds. Nor do I think point fourteen reflects "depression days." In the prosperous years of 1920–29, there was widespread discussion of "acquisitive and profit-motivated society." My own published writings, and also those of Roy Wood Sellars, published before 1929 are even more socially radical than point fourteen.

Oliver L. Reiser (Pittsburgh, Pennsylvania):

In the main the Manifesto still appears sound, enlightened, and forward-looking.

In the fifth proposition I would delete "or cosmic"; and I would delete proposition six entirely. I would change the emphasis of the whole Manifesto so that world citizenship in a planetary democracy would stand out. Loyalty to man as the planetary species is our highest loyalty.

I would add in proposition one or two, a more explicit statement of the meaning of "naturalism." Negatively, naturalism rules out supernaturalism (miracles) and also a mechanistic-materialistic view. Ethics now needs a cosmology, and pantheism provides a new plateau transcending the conflict of Marxist atheism and Christian supernaturalism.

Clinton Lee Scott (Boston, Massachusetts):

Except for some rephrasing to make the Manifesto a bit less dogmatic I would change nothing. Point fourteen will again be relevant. I wouldn't change it.

V. T. Thayer (Arlington, Virginia):

I would still be willing to sign the Manifesto. However, I am less convinced than in the 1930's that "In every field of human activity, the vital movement is in the direction of a candid and explicit humanism." There are too many drums sounding a retreat!

If I were to prepare such a statement today I would tone down expressions of dogmatism here and [t]here. Thus, in number six I would suggest "the time *has come* for a thorough *revision* of theism, deism . . ." rather than to say "the time has passed. . . ."

I would change number four so as to stress that the

individual is both molded by his culture and, as an active participant in it, can help to give form and character to his times.

Number nine should read not merely "co-operative effort to promote social well-being," but "finds his religious emotions expressed in fruitful living within the lives of others and in co-operative efforts to promote social well-being."

The first sentence of number fourteen requires re-writing in the present context. We should condemn both a profit-motivated society and a collectivist- and state-dominated society.

We should affirm our faith in a free intelligence. We oppose all attempts to cabin, crib, or confine the minds of men. We believe the health of a free society, as well as that of a free individual, is conditioned upon keeping open the channels of free inquiry. Only thus can men assure to themselves and their successors a perennial replenishment of the human spirit and the adequate utilization of resources, both physical and spiritual, essential to a good society.

E. C. Vanderlaan (San Francisco, California):

I am glad that there is to be a fresh look at the Humanist Manifesto. My comments (without at this moment being ready to frame the improved language I should desire) deal mainly with the following points:

1. *The opening paragraphs.* Here I would not insist that Humanism be called religion. I would state that Humanism is for *some* the essence of religion, while others regard it as a philosophy and central devotion which is, strictly speaking, an *equivalent* or *substitute* for religion. This might free us of the charge of currying favor by the misuse of language.

2. *Seventh affirmation.* In line with the above, this paragraph, while noble-sounding, is objectionable. If "religion" covers all human interests, the word has no distinctive meaning, and merely serves to impart (we hope) an air of good intentions to our declarations.

3. *Fourteenth affirmation.* Here we should make clear that Humanism is not bound by any economic dogma—neither Marxian theory nor the superstition that un-

restrained profit-hunting is productive of all good. Or say, Humanism holds that every political and economic system in the world is subject to impartial scrutiny and ethical appraisal.

4. In the light of present trends, we should strongly protest against the assumption, sometimes tacit but often implicit, that good citizenship is necessarily bound up with belief in traditional religious doctrines. For this means that the greatest questions which can engage human thought, are now to be removed from the field of open inquiry, and are to be answered once [and] for all by the authority of churches and the prejudices of the uninformed. No revised Manifesto should fail to deal sharply with this current phenomenon.

Jacob J. Weinstein (Chicago, Illinois):

Humanism is essentially a young man's faith. It is Promethean and therefore limited. How long can you shout defiance at the heavens? Life's slow strain finds it inadequate in situations of emotional stress. There are mysteries which cannot tolerate an agnostic answer. There are moments when the refusal to call upon the Friend behind phenomena leads to paralysis of the will. To accept only what the intellect clears makes for a glacial astringency of the blood. To refuse to personalize "the power not ourselves making for righteousness" leads to a sense of rootlessness and makes it almost impossible to communicate one's faith in moral integrity to his children. To accept the mytho-poetry of the classical religions does indeed open the door to superstitions and irrational binges of the emotions, but it is a chance we must take. Better to take it than to close the door on the tides of inspiration that bring us the profound and sustaining insights.

I have tried to resist the fears that come with the middle years. I have tried to detour the highway of "disillusion with science because it has not brought Utopia." I hope this is not a reaction of the jilted. But who can tell? Who can really penetrate to the true sources of one's judgment?

Nevertheless, I shall always be grateful to Humanism. It has, among other things, placed certain limits on the waywardness of the emotions. It has reigned in the heart and contributed toward that search for a synthesis of mind and heart which is the quest of every mature man.

David Rhys Williams (Rochester, New York):

Most of the ideas are still valid, but the language in which they are couched is deadly prosaic and unnecessarily uninspiring. It is like a scientifically built aeroplane, but without wings—it doesn't get off the ground. *The Declaration of Independence* is very concrete but it also possesses eloquence and literary power. The Manifesto needs rephrasing as much as anything.

In point five I would leave out "or cosmic." Does not "makes unacceptable any supernatural guarantees of human values" describe the Humanist position sufficiently? Are the "human values" outside the cosmos?

I would leave out point six entirely unless theism, deism, modernism, etc. are specifically defined. There are some whose theism doesn't seem to differ much from Humanism.

I would amend point fourteen by the addition suggested by the staff of *The Humanist* [quoted in A. J. Carlson's reply above].

I believe if the Manifesto is to be rewritten it should indicate some awareness of the atomic age in which we now live and have something to say about the peril to human values involved in the use of atomic weapons by any nation, including our own.

Edwin H. Wilson (Yellow Springs, Ohio):

I would prefer that we leave the Humanist Manifesto for what it has always been—a dated document representing a general agreement of thirty-four men at a particular moment in history. For today's purposes we need a new and fighting Humanist Declaration under whose banner we can lead a crusade for the freedoms across the country.

Point five in the present Manifesto seems to me insufficiently to show that, as Julian Huxley has put it, "man is the conscious agent of the evolutionary process." Although our values are not guaranteed by evolution, the need for them and the materials for their realization have all been determined in part by the process that has made man what he is.

Concerning point fourteen, if today many Humanists, including myself, are less sanguine about state ownership and operation of industry as a magic means of solving all our problems than we were in the great days of Norman Thomas' leadership, it is because we have seen what happens when the state gets too much power in its hands. The Humanist movement, however, should not be committed to any one specific economic answer. It would be enough to say that continued struggle by all Humanists to end poverty, disease, ignorance, and prejudice—the real sources of war and other international conflict—seems imperative.

In any new Humanist Declaration there should be a reaffirmation of the freedoms and adequate delineation of antidemocratic and anti-Humanist forces which threaten to destroy the democratic way of life here at home under the guise of protecting our security from alien forces abroad. McCarthyism; crypto-fascist attacks on the UN and UNESCO; clericalist pressures to invade our public schools; efforts to impose a theocratic basis of citizenship ("freedom *under God*"); the subversion of free, modern public education in behalf of a program of ritualistic indoctrination to favor a confluence of reactionary forces—all these need resisting with all the force we can muster.

The Symposium: Part II

The reappraisals by two manifesto signers—Dieffenbach and Dietrich—were received too late for publication in the first part of the symposium, so were included in the second part, which was published in the May/June 1953 issue of *The Humanist* (13:3:136–141). In addition, a number of persons who had by this time become actively involved in the humanist movement were invited to comment. They were Van Meter Ames, professor of philosophy at the University of Cincinnati; Fred G. Bratton, professor of literature and history of religion at Springfield College, Massachusetts; Harold Larrabee, professor of philosophy at Union College, Schenectady, New York; Alfred McClung Lee, a sociologist and president of the Unitarian Fellowship for Social Justice; Corliss Lamont, author of *The Illusion of Immortality* and *The Phi-*

losophy of Humanism; Francis Meyers, professor of philosophy at the University of Denver; Arthur E. Morgan, engineer,
Antioch College president, author, and active commentator
to our journal since 1933; Lloyd Morain, then president of
the American Humanist Association; Herbert J. Muller, professor at Purdue University in West Lafayette, Indiana (not
to be confused with Nobel laureate Hermann J. Muller, who
later became president of the AHA); Harold Scott, minister
of the Unitarian Church of Salt Lake City, Utah (and brother
of Clinton Lee Scott, manifesto signer); Mark Starr, the educational director for the International Ladies Garment Workers
Union; Gerald Wendt, the former editorial director of *Science
Illustrated* and, at the time, in charge of popular education
in the physical sciences for the United Nations Educational,
Scientific, and Cultural Organization (UNESCO); and
Gardner Williams, professor of philosophy at the University
of Toledo, Ohio.

The inclusion of these additional persons shows the
growth of the movement in the two decades following publication of the manifesto. These people represent the individualism
that inevitably is found in a movement practicing freedom
of inquiry, with no absolutes, creeds, or revelations to bind
its participants or inhibit critical thought. They were posed
with the same questions as the participants of Part I.

Van Meter Ames (Cincinnati, Ohio):

In several of the articles of the Manifesto the word "religion" is used, but not defined or delimited. On the contrary, as in Article 10, we are told there are "no uniquely
religious emotions and attitudes of the kind hitherto associated with belief in the supernatural." But what kind are
there now?

In fact I thought there was some question whether
Humanism should be considered a philosophy rather than
a religion. As long as no content is given to the word "religion," should it and its adjective be omitted from the Manifesto, as being question-begging and lacking in meaning?

I balk at Article 14. It gets into questions we have not
worked out and are united on. So far as it says anything
we all accept, hasn't it been covered by the preceding

points? With Norman Thomas going back on socialism, with capitalism being modified, this is a pretty difficult region to be sure of. A shared life in a shared world, yes; but as to the specific political or economic aspects of it, I wonder if we are technically qualified to take a definite stand. Here is something for social scientists and philosophers to work on; not for us as a sect to make a pronouncement.

Fred G. Bratton (Springfield, Massachusetts):

As over against the otherworldliness of traditional supernaturalism, the unreason of neo-orthodoxy, and the compromises of modernism, religious humanism stands as the most satisfactory realignment of religious thought for our day. And after two decades the Humanist Manifesto emerges as a fitting description of mature religion.

To become more specific in the Manifesto is to relate Humanism only to the present, to freeze it, so to speak. Therefore, I feel that the Manifesto, on the whole, is relevant without being dated.

The only possible addition I would suggest is this: as the common denominator of religion, Humanism emphasizes the ultimate ideal ends to be achieved in life rather than the incidental or instrumental means. To conceive religion in terms of universals rather than particulars, personal attitude rather than the observance of specific forms and beliefs, to see it as a qualitative whole rather than an isolated segment of life is to reach "the higher synthesis." This is Humanism.

Albert C. Dieffenbach (Cambridge, Massachusetts):

I have read the comments [of the other original signers] in the proofs, and I really have nothing to add to them.

It may be that a new Humanist declaration is desirable, as indicated in several of the comments, but my own feeling is that the original one may well stand, for is it likely that there could be agreement upon anything better?

In any case, I feel no interest in a revision of the Humanist Manifesto.

John H. Dietrich (Berkeley, California):

I do not have a copy of the Manifesto at hand, so cannot

comment on it in detail, but I think you are wise to let it stand as an historical document. It is definitely a dated instrument and represents what I have come to feel is a dated philosophy—a philosophy too narrow in its conception of great cosmic schemes, about which we know so little, and concerning which we should be less dogmatic and arrogant. It in no [way] reflects the humility which becomes the real seeker after truth. But that is the kind of fellows we were in those days. In fact, I was one of the chief offenders, and I confess it now in all humility. I see now that my utter reliance upon science and reason and my contempt for any intuitive insights and intangible values, which are the very essence of art and religion, was a great mistake. I think the Humanism of that period served a good purpose as a protest movement, but its day is passed. What I am trying to say is that the positive side of Humanism was and is fine—its insistence upon the enrichment of life in its every form; but its negative side, cutting itself off from all cosmic relationship, and denying or ignoring every influence outside of humanity itself, I think, was and is very shortsighted.

Corliss Lamont (New York, New York):

I believe that the Humanist Manifesto of 1933 was a landmark in the development of religious and philosophical Humanism. It is an historical document of great worth and importance in the Humanist movement and must be included as vital source material in any careful study of modern Humanism. Frank criticism of the Manifesto, however, must be the prelude to any new declaration of basic Humanist principles.

In my opinion the Humanist Manifesto's definition of religion is far too vague; and for this reason I would favor the omission of Point Seven altogether. In its place, in the preface, I suggest some such definition as this: "Religion is an integrated and inclusive way of life to which a group of persons give supreme commitment and which involves the shared quest of the ideal." At the same time I would not repeat the phrase "religious humanism" throughout the Manifesto, but would talk merely of "Humanism." In the preface, too, should be a statement that Humanism is "a religion or philosophy."

The First Point of the Manifesto I would rephrase as follows: "Humanism regards the universe as eternal, self-existing and uncreated, with no supernatural origins or destiny. This universe is dynamic in its very structure and is constantly changing in its every aspect."

To the Second Point I would add this sentence: "Man's inseparable unity of mind and body indicates that in all probability there is no personal survival after death."

Point Six should be revised as out of date, with "the several varieties of neo-orthodoxy" substituted for "modernism and the several varieties of new thought."

Point Fourteen, as I have been saying for many years, goes too far in involving Humanism in fundamental economic issues. Humanism as such should not claim to have solutions for all human problems or set itself up as a specific economics, political science, or sociology. In place of Point Fourteen, I think a new declaration might well state: "Humanism relies upon the use of intelligence and scientific method, applied with courage and vision, in the solution of all human problems—whether personal, social, economic, political, national, or international. The method of intelligence requires the further extension of conscious planning into the various realms of human endeavor."

Definite lacks in the Humanist Manifesto are its failure to state Humanism's ultimate ethical allegiance to the welfare and progress of all humanity, regardless of race, nationality, religion, sex, or occupation; its failure to include a separate plank on the achievement of international peace; its failure to mention the importance of art, beauty, and the appreciation of external nature; and its failure to give due significance to democracy and democratic procedures.

Regarding this last-mentioned deficiency, I would like to see some such formulation as this: "Humanism stands for the establishment of democracy in the fullest sense in every relevant sector of human life. It believes in the complete social implementation of reason and scientific method; and thereby in the use of democratic procedures, including freedom of speech and civil liberties, throughout all areas of political, economic, and cultural activity."

I consider very important the inclusion of a final point showing that Humanism is not dogmatic. Here I suggest: "Humanism, in accordance with the principles of science, believes in the unending questioning of basic assumptions and ideas, including its own. The Humanist viewpoint is a developing one which remains ever open to new facts and more rigorous reasoning, and which can never be restricted to any final formulation."

Harold A. Larrabee (Schenectady, New York):

As I have often written, the religious side of Humanism is what interests me least, and the least appetizing phase of it is the creedal or semicreedal. I think Humanism ought to try hard to avoid degenerating into "just another church" or "just another sect."

So my idea of a manifesto would be something you could get on a postcard. . . . I think anything else inevitably leads to signers versus nonsigners, orthodox versus heretics, *ad infinitum.*

There should be just two or three very broad principles which make you a Humanist or not—and the lines should *not* be precisely drawn.

Alfred McClung Lee (Thomaston, Connecticut):

Whether or not a manifesto might once have been appropriate for Humanism, in my estimation anything that might be called a manifesto is not appropriate for us now.

Humanists have in common chiefly an attitude toward belief and knowledge. We believe in the findings of science, subject to constant check, recheck, and modification. The findings of science come from the observation of natural phenomena—physical, biological, and social. Scientists state their findings in the simplest terms and theories that will fit available data. In terms of our evidence, this leaves no room for such dualism as body and spirit. Scientific evidence tells us nothing about spirits or gods as such. It deals with such nonworldly matters as artifacts.

Beyond this attitude, with its implicit distrust for dogmas and authoritarianism, there is room for many healthy disagreements. Even in the definition of this attitude, Humanists disagree and are likely to continue to do so.

Francis Meyers (Denver, Colorado):

I think the Manifesto is generally accurate to the spirit of

Humanism. But it also strikes me as being somewhat repetitious, pedestrian, and professional. There is a tendency for the basic issues to be lost in the enumeration of many points. The main suggestion, then, would be to reorganize the many separate parts into an eloquent, simple, direct, and clear statement of the meaning of religion and science, their relationships, and their significance for human affairs. This, I think, would make possible a more positive statement, and one which would eliminate such irrelevant and possibly misleading specifics as those contained in the first and fourteenth points. (I mean by this that the Humanist movement is not, as such, committed to any particular item of belief—as in the first point—nor to any particular social program—as in the fourteenth.)

Lloyd Morain (Cambridge, Massachusetts):

Rare though wonderful is the individual whose intellect is excited and whose heart is warmed by the Manifesto. In the early thirties the framers of the Manifesto, like most of us, were unaware of the full implications of the third way. For instance, they failed to make explicit the great simple difference between Humanism and traditional religions. The Humanist has a developing viewpoint. For him, scientific and critical methods are of primary importance. He has no place for the methods relied on by the traditional religionists who depend upon revelation, sacred books, and upon institutionalized religious authority. Humanism recognizes that knowledge is forever expanding, being revised, and cannot legitimately be bound by revelation or authority.

To me it is unfortunate that the framers of the Manifesto implied that religion is almost everything under the sun except possibly Mrs. MacGillicuddy's cooking of cabbage for dinner. In actual usage Humanism is the name applied to the general naturalistic viewpoint or orientation. It serves many people as a religion, others as a philosophy, and still others as a general social viewpoint—that is, men's relations with each other, with nature, and with society.

It may be "heresy" but from time to time I have wondered whether the publication of the Manifesto didn't set back the development of the Humanist movement. This is my opinion even though I am in general agreement with practically everything stated in the document.

Arthur E. Morgan (Yellow Springs, Ohio):

Twenty years ago I refrained from signing the Humanist Manifesto, for several reasons:

The first point, "Religious Humanists regard the universe as self-existing and not created," states a dogmatic position. I know of no conclusive evidence, pro or con.

Throughout the Manifesto *human* life is regarded as the sole end and aim of human concern. The assumption, by inference, that ours is the only organic species that can have significance, may, I think, have practical results that are far-reaching and harmful, in the thoughtless elimination of other species.

The fourteenth point, calling for a co-operative and socialized economic order, tends to commit Humanism to a special type of social structure. Given informed and disciplined good will, I believe that varied types of social structures may be equally beneficent.

Intelligence supplies the chart and compass of life, but emotion is the power plant. No religion or way of life will be fully effective unless it emphasizes education and nurture of the emotions in co-operation with intelligence. The lack of such definite emphasis in the Manifesto, and in the Humanist movement, is, I think, a serious defect. What the conventionally religious man calls "consecration" is analogous to a quality without which great human advance seldom occurs.

My chief reservation concerning the Manifesto was not for what it contained, most of which I agree with, but because of what was omitted. My hesitancy lay in the hope that a more eloquent pronouncement might be made.

Herbert J. Muller (Lafayette, Indiania):

Although I substantially agree with the Manifesto, I should boil it down considerably. A point-by-point manifesto looks too much like a creed—which you say it isn't. It is unlikely to make converts or even to unite Humanists, who are of many degrees and varieties. And do you really want something as aggressive in its connotations as a "manifesto"?

Harold Scott (Salt Lake City, Utah):

In rereading the Humanist Manifesto, I find it, in my judgment, surprisingly good—after all these years. Of course, it would be easy to find some fault with it—the seventh proposition gives a very sloppy definition of religion that might be tightened up a bit.

I note you mention something about [a revision of] point fourteen. It seems to me it is just as true as it ever was—and there is nothing in it that I can see that gives any aid and comfort to either Fascism or Sovietism.

Mark Starr (New York, New York):

The Manifesto has stood up remarkably to the test of time. Twenty years ago it was the economic depression. A disastrous Second World War has revealed extremes of bestiality and cruelty which have been used to "prove" that evil man is beyond redemption except by supernatural aid. Science has solved old problems and advanced new and complicated conceptions of "matter" and "energy" which have also been misused to support superhuman explanations or reliance on the "leap of faith" to accept what we cannot yet explain. We are also more aware since the fifth clause was drafted that science can be misused to the point of cosmic suicide.

For my part, point fourteen still holds. The motive of individual pecuniary profit remains inadequate. The suggested change to "a socialized and co-operative . . . order" is now no longer acceptable as a general panacea. The process of change has become more complicated in a simultaneous operation of *private* and *public* enterprise. Ideas about large-scale business and collectivism have been revised, but the emphasis of the common good remains paramount.

Gerald Wendt (Paris, France):

A brief comment on the Humanist Manifesto is not easy to write because the Manifesto is, for the most part, very good indeed and the suggested changes involve subtleties that are not easy to explain in few words, or, on the other hand, they involve whole new points of view that also need full statement to be comprehensible. But within the limits of your present interest and of my present time-allowance, I'd write something like this:

The Manifesto was certainly written by a small group of serious thinkers and apparently addressed to a group, not much larger, of the same. Its major defect is that it employs the language of professional philosophers, including many technical terms which are not understood outside the profession, and is therefore meaningful only within the profession. For this reason it is not a public manifesto at all but a credo for initiates. Hence a new manifesto is needed which may say the same but will say it in words of one syllable.

As for the individual points, I feel that the fifth is an inadequate and somewhat negative statement which should be revised to express a profound reliance on the research method for gaining reliable knowledge in the vast universe of truth that comprises not merely physical "realities" but biological, psychological, sociological and even spiritual truths as well.

And the fourteenth seems unwise, not because it is for the moment unpopular in the United States, but because it is too specific and conclusive and represents a passing phase of a local "culture pattern." This point instead should express faith in the abiding Christian (or not) virtue of good will toward *all* men, in the educability of all men, in the value of the democratic spirit and the desire of the Humanist to solve economic problems and revise economic theories, including establishing practices, with the same objective method and the same acceptance of new truths that have made the scientific revolution so inevitably successful.

Finally, what the Manifesto lacks is specific reference to other cultures than Western, other religions than Christian, other races than white. It should now be written as a true manifesto that appeals to the entire human race and that should provide a foundation for a new faith that will unite humankind.

Gardner Williams (Toledo, Ohio):

In many places its language is unintelligible to persons who have not studied philosophy or who have not studied Dewey. By adhering narrowly to Dewey it ignores the larger insights of Santayana and other sound naturalistic thinkers. Actually the dualism of physical substance and conscious experience is basic in the theory of knowledge. These are not two substances, but they are two things, substance and attribute. All science indicates that consciousness depends upon the nervous system and is tied down to its neurons. It is not possible for men to share their experiences.

Almost nobody will know what is meant by the assertion that man must face the crises of life in terms of his knowledge of their naturalness and their probability. No connection is shown between their naturalness and their probability. Few people know what "their probability" means, or what "in terms of" means.

Prayer, as practiced in many liberal Unitarian churches, is a rededication of the self to ultimate ideals. This should not be disparaged.

The modernism of Santayana is based upon a thoroughgoing naturalism and Humanism. It expresses a more profound wisdom in matters of religion than Dewey ever possessed.

Socialism is no part of Humanist doctrine.

The unqualified assertion that man has the power to realize the world of his dreams is false optimism. Man can only partly realize this world anyhow, and all his hopes may be shattered. Let us try to realize as much as possible. But Reinhold Niebuhr can ridicule this false optimism powerfully by appealing to obvious facts.

CHAPTER 18

The Manifesto's
Long-Term Impact

O ver the decades since 1933, the radical nature of "A Humanist Manifesto" continued to be a source of controversy. Among the long-term effects of the manifesto, perhaps one of the most significant is the generation of a second manifesto in 1973. The forty interim years saw dramatic cultural and socioeconomic changes. Collectively, we are still trying to cope with them as technology continues to race ahead of our ability to assign meaning to our lives.

The second manifesto—*Humanist Manifesto II*—was published in the September/October 1973 issue of *The Humanist* (XXIII:5:4–9). The preface to that version, for which I was recognized as editor emeritus, follows. It indicates some of the flaws of the first manifesto and offers some of the reasons for producing a second:

> It is forty years since *Humanist Manifesto I* (1933) appeared. Events since then make that earlier statement seem far too optimistic. Nazism has shown the depths of brutality of which humanity is capable. Other totalitarian regimes have suppressed human rights without ending poverty. Science has sometimes brought evil as well as good. Recent decades have shown that inhuman wars can be made in the name of peace. The beginnings of police states, even in democratic societies, widespread government espionage, and other abuses of power by military, political, and industrial elites, and the continuance of

unyielding racism, all present a different and difficult social outlook. In various societies, the demands of women and minority groups for equal rights effectively challenge our generation.

As we approach the twenty-first century, however, an affirmative and hopeful vision is needed. Faith, commensurate with advancing knowledge, is also necessary. In the choice between despair and hope, humanists respond in this *Humanist Manifesto II* with a positive declaration for times of uncertainty.

As in 1933, humanists still believe that traditional theism, especially faith in the prayer-hearing God, assumed to love and care for persons, to hear and understand their prayers, and to be able to do something about them, is an unproved and outmoded faith. Salvationism, based on mere affirmation, still appears as harmful, diverting people with false hopes of heaven hereafter. Reasonable minds look to other means for survival.

Those who sign *Humanist Manifesto II* disclaim that they are setting forth a binding credo; their individual views would be stated in widely varying ways. This statement is, however, reaching for vision in a time that needs direction. It is social analysis in an effort at consensus. New statements should be developed to supersede this, but for today it is our conviction that humanism offers an alternative that can serve present-day needs and guide humankind toward the future.

Since the publication of *Humanist Manifesto II*, literally thousands of signatures have been collected—and the process is ongoing.

Misuse of *Manifesto I*

As with any controversial statement, the humanist manifesto of 1933 has been taken out of context and misused—sometimes as a result of simple carelessness but occasionally for deliberate purpose of propaganda.

One of the most common misunderstandings about the manifesto is its identification as a humanist creed. It was never intended as a doctrine—a point the originators were clear about, as we've seen from their numerous correspondence included in this book. In addition, the manifesto was published in the May/June 1933 issue of *The New Humanist* with a specific disclaimer and, with rare exceptions, its subsequent publications have included it, as they ought.

In 1969, Dr. Max Rafferty, superintendent of public instruction of the California State Board of Education, published a special seventy-four-page report entitled "Guidelines for Moral Instruction in California Schools," in which almost half of its pages criticize "the challenge of secular humanism" and indict the manifesto. Rafferty attempted to blame humanism, humanists (including John Dewey), and progressive education in general for the decline of "morality" among America's youth. While the humanist philosophy is certainly one that comports well with social reform and innovation, it neither created nor can be held responsible for all social change. Despite this obvious fact, humanism has been made the scapegoat for "evil" in much of modern Christian apologetics. In the case of Dr. Rafferty, the strategy backfired. So much protest resulted from his report that it was ultimately put on file as accepted but not approved. A replacement report that left out the attack on humanism was later published.

Another example of a misrepresentation of the manifesto comes from a publication called *Imprimus*, the journal of Hillsdale College's two conservative seminar programs: the Center for Constructive Alternatives and the Shavano Institute for National Leadership. Located in Hillsdale, Michigan, the former program is open to students and the public; the latter program, while also public, is offered in different cities around the country each year. High-profile, conservative speakers conduct the seminars on various topics of public policy.

Imprimus, with a current circulation of 600,000, reproduces the speeches of the seminar speakers. In the March 1975 issue, James T. McKenna, the general counsel to the Heritage Foundation, laments over public education and its role as a major player in "the total picture of collapse which now confronts the American parent and taxpayer." In laying out the explanation for his thorough disdain of public education, McKenna refers to the "insatiable appetite of the state for control over the family unit and the child" and "the dehumanizing of human relationships and the desacralization of the human being as the repository of an irreducible dignity." As examples of this desacralization, he uses both the 1933 and the 1973 humanist manifestos:

> The final blow to parental and public confidence in education was the substitution of value systems based on ethical opportunism and the shallow paganism of Humanist Manifesto I and II.
>
> It is not accidental that the most prestigious educator of the Twentieth Century, the teacher of teachers should have been a principal shaper of the first Humanist Manifesto in 1933. John Dewey spoke for the priorities of educators, "Faith in a loving caring God, is an unproved and outmoded faith."

As we have seen, John Dewey was not a principal shaper of *Humanist Manifesto I* but simply one of its signers. In fact, Dewey made no editorial comments at all. His name is constantly invoked only because he was, beyond question, the most famous signer and an important and guiding influence on today's educators.

Like Rafferty in California, who assigned humanists and humanism the responsibility for moral decline, McKenna attributes the manifestos with the power to strike the "final blow" to public confidence in the educational system.

The decade of the 1980s saw a concerted and organized attack on humanism by the religious right wing. Televangelists such as Jerry Falwell, Pat Robertson, Jim Bakker, and Jimmy Swaggart made humanism and the manifestos household words. Evangelist Tim LaHaye's *The Battle for the Mind*, published in 1980, in which the manifestos are called a "religious and philosophical bible," was probably the largest-selling anti-humanist book to hit the market.

In 1983, another author, Marlin Maddoux (then the host of a popular daily radio talk show, "Point of View," broadcast nationally over the Satellite Radio Network), wrote his own book, *Humanism Exposed*, warning readers that humanists "intend to transform society into a humanistic one with the religion of that new society being *Humanism*." In defending his warning cry to Christians that humanists intend "to bring about a one-world, socialistic, anti-God society," Maddoux quotes heavily from *Humanist Manifesto I and II*. He also offers interpretations of the manifestos that can only be described as gross exaggerations. Maddoux explains that the careful design of a humanist takeover includes control of America's educational system and the media. Of the former, he says: "I had to admit that the humanists' most ingenious move was the systematic takeover of the public school system in America. It showed a special insight, marked by originality, cleverness and clearness of purpose, and was the most important step toward turning an entire nation away from its original goals to the new goals set forth by organized humanism as articulated for us in Humanist Manifestos I and II." Interestingly, Maddoux's book was published in 1984 under a new name, *America Betrayed*, by a different publisher.

Those same years—1983 and 1984—saw further diatribes against humanism and the manifestos. In booklets published by the Institute in Basic Youth Conflicts in Oak Brook, Illinois (which now operates under the name Institute in Basic Life Principles), the editors offer their notation to *Humanist Manifesto I*. While many people would view their interpretations as ridiculous, they were and continue to be the common arguments of fundamental Christians against the "threat" of secular humanist domination. Point twelve of *Humanist Manifesto I* is a prime example. It reads: "Believing that religion must work increasingly for joy in living, religious humanists aim to foster the creative in man and to encourage achievements that add to the satisfactions of life." In *Applying Basic Principles*, the last three words are underlined and elaborated with the footnote: "Including any form of sexual perversion."

Such misinterpretations and exaggerations continue even today. In fact, *Manifesto I*'s statement in point six—that the time for theism, deism . . . has passed—continues to provoke and threaten some conservative Christians some sixty years after its original publication. I believe this is a testament to the boldness of the document.

Humanism Among the Quakers

As mentioned earlier in this book, the liberal religions were a breeding ground for humanism, and the Society of Friends (Quakers) was no exception. Sometime between 1937 and 1942, a brief but pointed memorandum entitled "To the Scientifically Minded," was published by the Advancement Committee of the Friends General Conference in Philadelphia. The complete text reads:

> For a large number of people of Christendom, especially for those trained in scientific thinking, the great organized Christian churches are failing to supply the needed religious element. The trend of our time is scientific. It is impossible for a religion which ignores or opposes this tendency to serve the purposes of all who receive modern education.
>
> Most of the churches through their official bodies insist upon the Apostles or the Nicene Creed, the inerrancy of the Bible, the virgin birth of Jesus, and the verity of the miracle stories of the old and new Testament, as essentials of belief. This letter is not addressed to those who are satisfied with such a creed; it is rather for any who have not found religious satisfaction.
>
> This letter calls your attention to the Religious Society of Friends, commonly called Quakers. This society makes no claim to be a church in the sense of assuming authority to settle questions of doctrine or of historic fact. We are a *society of friends* whose members owe each other friendliness, and claim no authority one over another. We have no formal creed, and such unity as we have—and we have a great deal—is due to the fact that reasonable minds working on the same materials are likely to arrive at similar conclusions. However, we demand no unity of opinion and we find both interest and stimulus in our many differences.
>
> Most Friends agree that the Sermon on the Mount presents the highest ideal for a way of life; this we accept not only on authority from without but mainly as conviction from within. We thus unite on a common purpose; a human society organized on a basis of good will and friendliness.
>
> The Religious Society of Friends is a group of people

of good will, working together for mutual support in making the God element of life the commanding element. We never altogether succeed in doing this, but the effort is an essential part of our religion. It is only by squarely facing what *is* that many may hope to accomplish what *may be:* wherefore religion as we understand it has nothing to fear from science. Indeed we welcome every extension of mental horizon, every new discovery as to the nature of the world we live in.

We believe there are many who would find a richer life in membership with us, and we know that we need the strength of larger numbers. We need too the fellowship of men and women of intelligence and courage.

We invite correspondence with any of the signers of this letter at Friends' Advancement Committee, 1515 Cherry Street, Philadelphia, Pa.

The memorandum was signed by Jesse H. Holmes, professor emeritus of philosophy at Swarthmore College; Roscoe Pound, a professor at the University of Harvard College; Paul H. Douglas, professor of economics at the University of Chicago; J. Russell Smith, professor of economic geography at Columbia University; and Albert T. Mills, professor of history and political science at James Millikin University.

We can see essentially the same influence at work among the Quakers—a drift in the culture toward religious naturalism —as was at work among the Unitarians, Universalists, and Ethical Culturists.

It is interesting that, just as the humanists' manifesto disavowed creedal intentions in 1933, so did the Friends' Advancement Committee. Furthermore, among Quakers as among Unitarians, the influence of science and the scientific method prompted a public declaration.

Also comparable to "A Humanist Manifesto" is the obvious trouble that the Quakers were experiencing with god language and its implied theism. These members of the Society of Friends did not, as in the almost contemporary humanist manifesto of 1933, disclaim theism, but they did give it a modernist new-wine-in-old-bottles meaning. Significantly, their memorandum affirms that "reasonable minds at work on the same materials are likely to arrive at similar conclusions."

There were, however, other Quakers who were more forthrightly humanist. In Yellow Springs, Ohio, the Society of Friends had long accepted members with frankly natural-istic (non-Christian, nontheistic) philosophies, among whom were Dr. Arthur E. Morgan and his son Ernest (who actually served for a time on the board of directors of the American Humanist Association).

The philosophical conflict between Christians and non-theists inevitably led some Quaker humanists to break away from the fold altogether. One group, led by Dr. Lowell H. Coate, established the Cooperative Friends Society on July 5, 1939, at a weekend conference of the First Universalist Church of Los Angeles, California. At that conference, Dr. George T. Ashley, a humanist Unitarian minister, formally ordained the principal leaders of the new society, thereby guar-anteeing that their ministerial status could never be challenged. Later that same year, on December 16, the group officially changed its name to the Humanist Society of Friends.

Early in its history, the HSOF came to rely on *Humanist Manifesto I*. The group's "Official Statement of Principles" in the 1940s reprinted the manifesto in its entirety and de-clared that it "represented the Humanist Society of Friends' general philosophy of Religion."

Over the years, the HSOF brought into its leadership people not only of Quaker background but of other religious traditions as well. And it attracted educators and scholars, business and labor leaders, artists and scientists, professionals and others from many walks of life. The society conducted religious meetings and conferences and performed various rites of passage for its members. For a time, it published an official magazine, the *Humanist Friend*, and conducted a Humanist Friends College in connection with De Landis University.

In 1987, the HSOF became a chartered chapter of the American Humanist Association and, in 1990, an incorporated division responsible for the AHA's ministerial and other reli-gious humanist programs.

A Final Note

To the extent that it is an expression of concern for humanity in the here and now, I am proud of my involvement in the creation of the 1933 *Humanist Manifesto.* All these years later, I still view the collection of its thirty-four signatures to be an accomplishment. It also helped me to meet one of my goals as an early advocate of humanism in that it provided a bridge between liberal theologists and philosophers, further embellished by the approval of people from other areas of academia and other professions.

Because the manifesto was not written to be a creed or doctrine, humanist thinking has been able to evolve freely over time. Though *Manifesto I* reiterates the hopefulness that socialism brought to the 1930s, in retrospect I think humanism should not attach itself to any particular economic system. However, as both a religion and a philosophy, it should continue to commit itself to ending poverty, disease, ignorance, and prejudice.

Upon rereading *Humanist Manifesto I,* its naivete is clear. Equally clear, however, are the ways in which the document has transcended the past six decades. I can still happily affirm almost all of its theses.

Bibliography

Ames, Edward Scribner. 1949. *Religion.* Chicago, IL: John O. Pyle (also, New York, NY: Henry Holt and Company, 1929).

———. 1919. *The Psychology of Religious Experience.* Boston, MA: Houghton Mifflin Company.

Ames, Van Meter (editor). *Prayers and Meditations.* 1970. Chicago, IL: The Disciples' Divinity House, University of Chicago.

Applying Basic Principles. 1983. Oak Brook, IL: booklet published by the Institute in Basic Youth Conflicts.

Auer, J. A. C. F. 1933. *Humanism States Its Case.* Boston, MA: Beacon Press.

Auer, J. A. C. F., and Hart, Julian. 1952. *Humanism Versus Theism.* Yellow Springs, OH: The Antioch Press).

Axtelle, George E. 1967. "John Dewey's Concept of 'The Religious.'" *Religious Humanism* (Summer) 1:3:65–68.

Bahm, Archie J. 1953. "A Religious Affirmation." *The Humanist* (March/April) XIII:2:48.

Bentley, Arthur F. 1954. *Inquiry into Inquiries.* Boston, MA: Beacon Press.

Bestic, Alan. 1971. *Praise the Lord and Pass the Contribution.* London: Cassell Books (also New York, NY: Taplinger Publications).

Black, Algernon (contributing editor). 1933. *The Standard* (August) 19:221.

Bragg, Raymond. 1953. "An Historical Note." *The Humanist* (March/April) XIII:2:62–63.

Bullert, Gary. 1983. *The Politics of John Dewey.* Buffalo, NY: Prometheus Books.

Burtt, E. A. 1939. *Types of Religious Philosophy.* New York, NY: Harper and Brothers.

Darrow, Clarence. 1934. *The Story of My Life.* New York, NY: Charles Scribner's Sons.

Dewey, John. 1920. *Reconstruction in Philosophy.* New York, NY: Henry Holt and Company.

———. 1934. *A Common Faith.* New Haven, CT: Yale University Press.

Dietrich, John. 1927–1934. *The Humanist Pulpit.* Minneapolis, MN: The First Unitarian Society (out of print).

Doan, Frank Carlton. 1909. *Religion and the Modern Mind.* Boston, MA: Sherman, French, and Company.

Edman, Irwin. 1938. *Philosopher's Holiday.* New York, NY: The Viking Press.

Edwards, Paul (editor). 1967. *The Encyclopedia of Philosophy.* New York, NY: The Macmillan Company.

Einstein, Albert. 1950, 1983. *Essays in Humanism.* New York, NY: Philosophical Library.

Everett, Walter Goodnow. 1918. *Moral Values.* New York, NY: Henry Holt and Company.

Firkins, Oscar. 1931. "The Two Humanisms: A Discrimination." *The Humanist* (March/April) IV:3:1–9.

Foerster, Norman (editor). 1930. *Humanism and America.* New York, NY: Farrar and Rinehart, Inc.

Foster, George Burman. 1909. *The Function of Religion in Man's Struggle for Existence.* Chicago, IL: University of Chicago Press.

Grasso, James V. 1951. "Humanism in the Eighteenth Century." *The Humanist* (July/August) XI:4:175–176.

Grattan, C. Hartley. 1930. *The Critique of Humanism.* New York, NY: Brewer and Warren, Inc.

Griggs, Edward Howard. 1902. *The New Humanism: Studies in Personal and Social Development.* New York, NY: B. W. Huebsch (fourth edition; also New York, NY: Orchard Hill Press, 1922, eighth edition).

Hankins, F. H. 1908. *Studies in the Social Sciences.* New York, NY: Columbia University Studies in the Social Sciences.

Hart, James H. 1933. "A Religious Mood." *The New Humanist* (January/February) VI:1:1–9.

Hodgin, E. Stanton. 1948. *Confessions of an Agnostic Clergyman.* Boston, MA: Beacon Press.

Holloway, Rupert. 1933. "The Mystical Mood." *The New Humanist* (May/June) VI:3:14–18.

Hook, Sidney. 1967. Quoted by Sherwin T. Wine in *Religious Humanism* (winter) 1:1.

How to Understand Humanism. 1983. Oak Brook, IL: booklet published by the Institute in Basic Youth Conflicts.

"A Humanist Manifesto." 1933. *The New Humanist* (May/June) VI:3:1–5.

"Humanist Manifesto II." 1973. *The Humanist* (September/October) XXIII:5:4–9.

Hutcheon, Robert J. 1929. *Frankness in Religion.* (New York, NY: The Macmillan Company.

————. 1931. *Humanism in Religion Examined.* Chicago, IL: Meadville Theological School.

James, William. 1903. *Varieties of Religious Experience: A Study in Human Nature.* New York, Bombay, and London: Longman's Green and Company.

Kallen, Horace A. 1927. *Why Religion?* New York, NY: Boni and Liveright.

————. 1933. *Individualism—An American Way of Life.* New York, NY: Liveright, Inc.

————. 1947. *Freedom and Experience.* Ithaca, NY: Cornell University Press.

————. 1948. *Ideals and Experience.* Ithaca, NY: Cornell University Press.

————. 1951. *Democracy's True Religion.* Boston, MA: Beacon Press.

————. 1952. *Freedom in the Modern World.* Ithaca, NY: Cornell University Press.

————. 1959. *A Study of Liberty.* Yellow Springs, OH: The Antioch Press.

————. 1971. *What I Believe and Why—Maybe.* New York, NY: Horizon Press.

Kent, Gordon. 1944. *Humanism: Religion of the Post War World.* Denver, CO: privately published).

————. 1952. *Humanism for the Millions.* Yellow Springs, OH: American Humanist Association (third edition revised).

Knight, Frank. 1929. "Absolutism or Absolutism!" *The New Humanist* (May) II:2:1–3.

LaHaye, Tim. 1980. *The Battle for the Mind.* Old Tappan, NJ: Fleming H. Revell Company.

Lamont, Corliss. 1936. *Man Answers Death: An Anthology of Poetry.* New York, NY: G. P. Putnam's Sons (first edition; also New York, NY: Philosophical Library, 1952, second edition).

————. 1942. *Freedom Is As Freedom Does.* New York, NY: Da Capo Press.

————. 1949. *Humanism As a Philosophy.* New York, NY: Philosophical Library.

————. 1949. *The Philosophy of Humanism.* New York, NY: Frederick Ungar Publishing Company (first edition).

————. 1970. *A Humanist Wedding Service.* Buffalo, NY: Prometheus Books.

————. 1974. *Voice in the Wilderness.* Buffalo, NY: Prometheus Books.

————. 1977. *A Humanist Funeral Service.* Buffalo, NY: Prometheus Books.

————. 1981. *Yes to Life—Memoirs of Corliss Lamont.* New York, NY: Horizon Press.

Law, David A.; Angeles, Peter A.; Lamont, Corliss. 1968. "Dewey's Idea of the Religious—Critical Evaluations." *Religious Humanism* (winter) 11:1:25–26.

Lippmann, Walter. 1929. *A Preface to Morals.* New York, NY: Charles Scribner's Sons.

Lyttle, Charles H. 1952. *Freedom Moves West.* Boston, MA: Beacon Press.

Maddoux, Marlin. 1983. *Humanism Exposed.* Dallas, TX: Cornerstone Publishers.

———. 1984. *America Betrayed.* Shreveport, LA: Huntington House, Inc.

Maslow, Abraham H. 1964. *Religions, Values, and Peak Experiences.* Columbus, OH: Ohio State University Press (also New York, NY: The Viking Press, Inc., 1970).

———. 1970. "Religious Values and Peak Experiences." *Religious Humanism* 4:100–103.

Mondale, R. Lester. 1946. *Three Unitarian Philosophies of Religion.* Boston, MA: Beacon Press (also 1952).

———. 1973. *The New Man of Religious Humanism.* Peterhead, Scotland: Volturna Press.

Morain, Lloyd, and Morain, Mary. 1992. "Reminiscences of IHEU's Founding from the U.S.A." *International Humanist* (July):6–7.

More, Paul Elmer. 1936. *On Being Human* (volume III of the *New Shelbourne Essays.* Princeton, NJ: Princeton University Press (also London: Humphrey Milford, Oxford University Press).

Morgan, Arthur E. 1927. *My World.* Yellow Springs, OH: Kahoe and Spieth.

———. 1955. *Search for Purpose.* Yellow Springs, OH: The Antioch Press.

———. 1970. *Dams and Other Disasters.* Boston, MA: Porter Sargent.

Myers, Francis. 1967. "Comments on George Axtelle's 'John Dewey's Concept of the Religious.'" *Religious Humanism* (summer) 1:3:69–70.

Otto, Max Carl. 1924. *Things and Ideals.* New York, NY: Henry Holt and Company.

———. 1926. *Natural Laws and Human Hopes* (New York, NY: Henry Holt and Company (also Denver, CO: Alan Swallow, 1957, second edition).

———. 1949. *Science and the Moral Life.* New York, NY: The New American Library, A Mentor Book (fifth edition).

Parke, David B. 1957. *The Epic of Unitarianism.* Berkeley, CA: Starr King Press.

Persons, Stow. 1947. *Free Religion: An American Faith.* New Haven, CT: Yale University Press (also Boston, MA: Beacon Press, 1963).

Potter, Charles Francis. 1930. *Humanism: A New Religion.* New York, NY: Simon and Schuster (out of print).

———. 1933. *Humanizing Religion.* New York and London: Harper and Brothers Publishers.

Reese, Curtis W. 1926. *Humanism.* Chicago, IL: Open Court Publishing Company.

———. 1927. *Humanist Sermons.* Chicago, IL: Open Court Publishing Company (out of print).

———. 1931. *Humanist Religion.* New York, NY: The Macmillan Company.

———. 1945. *The Meaning of Humanism.* Boston, MA: Beacon Press (also Buffalo, NY: Prometheus Books, 1972).

Reisman, David. 1950. *The Lonely Crowd.* New Haven, CT: Yale University Press, Studies in National Policy.

Robertson, John B. (editor). 1905. *Philosophical Works of Francis Bacon.* New York, NY: E. P. Dutton and Company.

Robinson, James Harvey. 1921. *The Mind in the Making.* New York, NY: Harper Brothers Publishers.

———. 1924. *The Humanizing of Knowledge.* New York, NY: George H. Doran Company (also 1926).

Schiller, F. C. S. 1903. *Humanism: Philosophical Essays.* New York, NY: The Macmillan Company (also London: Macmillan and Company, Limited, 1912).

———. 1910. *Riddles of the Sphinx: A Study in the Philosophy of Humanism.* London: Macmillan and Company, Limited.

———. 1912. *Studies in Humanism.* London: Macmillan and Company, Limited.

———. 1924. *Tantalus.* New York, NY: E. P. Dutton and Company.

Schneider, Herbert W. 1964. *Religion in Twentieth Century America.* New York, NY: Atheneum.

Schultz, William. 1975. *Making the Manifesto: A History of Early Religious Humanism.* Chicago, IL: Meadville/Lombard Theological School doctoral dissertation.

Sellars, Roy Wood. 1918. *The Next Step in Religion.* New York, NY: The Macmillan Company.

———. 1922. *Evolutionary Naturalism.* Chicago, IL: Open Court Publishing Company.

———. 1928. *Religion Coming of Age.* New York, NY: The Macmillan Company.

———. 1932. *The Philosophy of Physical Realism.* New York, NY: The Macmillan Company.

———. 1933. "Religious Humanism." *The New Humanist* (May/June) VI:3:7–12.

———. 1933. "In Defense of the Manifesto." *The New Humanist* (May/June) VI:6:7–12.

Shipley, Maynard. 1927. *The Key to Evolution.* Girard, KS: Haldeman-Julius.

———. 1929. *The War on Modern Science.* New York, NY: A. A. Knopf.

Smith, Thomas Vernor. 1926. *The Democratic Way of Life.* Chicago, IL: The University of Chicago Press.

———. 1934. *Beyond Conscience.* New York, NY: Whittlesey House, McGraw Hill Book Company, Inc.

———. 1934. *Creative Skeptics*. Chicago and New York: Willett, Clark, and Company.

———. 1959. *The Ethics of Compromise*. Boston, MA: Starr King Press.

"A Symposium—A Look at the Humanist Manifesto Twenty Years After." 1953. *The Humanist* (March/April) XIII:2:58–71.

"A Symposium—Comments on the Humanist Manifesto." 1953. *The Humanist* (May/June) XIII:3:136–141.

Voss, Carl Hermann. 1980. *Rabbi and Minister: The Friendship of Stephen S. Wise and John Hayne Holmes*. Buffalo, NY: Prometheus Books.

Walker, Joseph. 1932. *Humanism As a Way of Life*. New York, NY: The Macmillan Company.

Wilson, Edwin H. 1930. "A New Synthesis: Among the Intellectuals." *The New Humanist*. (January) III:2:9–10.

———. 1930. "A New Synthesis: The Development of Method in Cooperative Problem Solving." *The New Humanist* (February) III:3:9–10.

———. 1930. "A New Synthesis: The Organization of Knowledge." *The New Humanist* (March) III:4:8–10.

———. 1930. "A New Synthesis: Integrating Science." *The New Humanist* (April) III:5:12–13.

———. 1930. "A New Synthesis: Adult Education, England." *The New Humanist* (May) III:6:12–13.

———. 1930. "A New Synthesis: Adult Education, the United States." *The New Humanist* (June) III:7:6–9.

———. 1991. "The Origins of Modern Humanism." *The Humanist* (January/February) LI:1:9.